Series / Number 01-063

Party, State, and Bureaucracy
in Western Germany

KENNETH H. F. DYSON
University of Liverpool

D1526325

⑤ SAGE PUBLICATIONS / Beverly Hills / London

For information address:

SAGE PUBLICATIONS, INC.
275 South Beverly Drive
Beverly Hills, California 90212

SAGE PUBLICATIONS LTD
28 Banner Street
London EC1Y 8QE

International Standard Book Number 0-8039-0758-3

Library of Congress Catalog Card No. L.C. 77-87567

FIRST PRINTING

When citing a professional paper, please use the proper form. Remember to cite the correct Sage Professional Paper series title and include the paper number. One of the two following formats can be adapted (depending on the style manual used):

(1) NAMENWIRTH, J. Z. and LASSWELL, H. D. (1970) "The Changing Language of American Values." Sage Professional Papers in Comparative Politics, 1, 01-001. Beverly Hills and London: Sage Pubns.

OR

(2) Namenwirth, J. Zvi and Lasswell, Harold D. 1970. *The Changing Language of American Values.* Sage Professional Papers in Comparative Politics, vol. 1, series no. 01-001. Beverly Hills and London: Sage Publications.

CONTENTS

Introduction 5

Party and State in Western Germany 8
  The Imperative Mandate Controversy 11
  Abuse of the Bundesrat? 15
  The "Party Book" Administration 20
  "Verfilzung" and the Social Structure of Parties
    and Parliament 37
  The "Party Book" Broadcasting Corporations 50
  The Dangers of the Party State 55

Party State and Elite Accommodation 59

Notes 65

References 67

Party, State, and Bureaucracy in Western Germany

KENNETH H. F. DYSON
University of Liverpool

INTRODUCTION

It has become commonplace to stress the importance of legalism and federalism as factors explaining many of the peculiar characteristics of West German government and bureaucracy. Certainly no analysis of that political system can overlook the implications of a constitutional commitment to the *Rechtsstaat* and the *Bundesstaat* in the Basic Law and of their reinforcement by German historical experience. A decentralized political structure and a normative conception of law combined with a formidable array of judicial controls have a profound effect on German policy making and administration. And yet the party political environment has tended to be neglected. There has been interest in the electoral and coalition politics of party (Burkett, 1975) but too little attention to the peculiar nature of German parties compared to their Anglo-Saxon equivalents. This neglect stems from a failure by Anglo-American scholars to identify the state as a significant conceptual variable of contemporary importance in the analysis of European political systems (but see Nettl, 1968). It can can be argued that compared to France or even Britain, party is particularly important for analysis of the policy process and bureaucratic behavior.

In German history the complex of party, state, and bureaucracy has presented major problems. Identification of state and bureaucracy has

AUTHOR'S NOTE: *I am especially indebted to Professor Uwe Thaysen for his assistance with my research during the preparation of this paper. He is, of course, not responsible for the specific interpretations herein. A research grant from the University of Liverpool helped defray some of the costs of this research. Finally, my special thanks to Ann and Charles.*

traditionally been at the expense of the authority of the parties. Today the term *Parteienstaat* (party state)—whatever disputes there may be about its contents—reflects a drastic alteration of relationships. Party permeates institutional life. At the same time democratization and pluralism have not meant the death of the state. The state has been transformed and is disseminated throughout public life with major consequences for the parties and more generally for the pluralistic process. German politics and bureaucratic behavior are only to be understood in terms of the state, and one crucial aspect of the contemporary state is a highly developed concept of party in the form of the Parteienstaat. A common weakness of the Almond (1956), Easton (1953), and Riggs (1964) approaches, and of political sociology generally, is underestimation of this dimension in comparative analysis.

In retrospect it may be possible to judge that the rise and fall of the Third Reich destroyed the basis of the traditional social and political order in Germany at least as effectively as the earlier English and French revolutions had done in these two states (Dahrendorf, 1968: 402-418). The consequences of the Second World War—refugees and expellees—led to a further displacement of the traditional social structure. In such a context postwar politics developed in a different way to the Weimar period. Restorative tendencies apparent in the 1950s were largely in the area of values and norms; they did not extend to the formation of counter-elites to the parties. Whereas it is possible to identify alternative elite formations to party in Britain (the Establishment) or France (the *grand corps*), it is much more difficult to do the same for Western Germany. There, as in Austria, the parties dominate political life. Rather than being just one aspect of a complex political order, they are recognized to play the key role in pluralistic politics. Likewise, they dominate administrative life. In Britain patronage was historically Crown patronage and its removal was a natural counterpart of the establishment of parliamentary supremacy; in Germany party patronage was the democratic response to the historical problem of the state. The Crown was related to democracy in Britain by political neutralization of the bureaucracy; the state was related to democracy in Germany by party politicization of the bureaucracy. Indeed much of the contemporary authority of the parties comes from the fact that they have inherited features of the state tradition (Ellwein, 1973: 174). As a consequence the state was never the same aloof detached and independent entity again and the parties took on peculiar qualities.

The collapse of the traditional elites and the discrediting of so many institutions by the Nazi period enabled the parties to play a strategic role in the formative years of postwar Germany. For example, they dominated the Parliamentary Council of 1948-1949. According to Wilhelm Hennis (1973: 79), "never before in German history has a constitution (the Basic Law) been drawn up in an assembly so completely dominated by party men." It was the parties and parliamentarians rather than the bureaucracy or the old military corps which filled the "power vacuum" at the beginning of the Federal Republic first at the local, then state, and finally federal levels. Surprisingly there was no reaction to the historical weakness of party in the German political tradition. The traditional doctrine of the state had relegated them to a subordinate role as articulators of interest, as parts of "society" rather than instruments of government. During the Weimar period Parteienstaat had been a term of abuse. Now an attempt was made to remedy past mistakes by rehabilitating them. Significantly the first article of the Basic Law dealing with West Germany's political institutions gave parties constitutional recognition for the first time. According to Article 21, "the parties shall participate in forming the political will of the people." The Party Law of 1967 not only recognized and regulated state finance for the parties' electoral activites but also endowed them with such wide functions as political education and "influencing political development." Gerhard Leibholz's (1967) thesis that they are "crypto-state" organs has been partly accepted by the Federal Constitutional Court which also formulated the doctrine of "party privilege" to protect party activities from interference by governments.

The new links forged between executive and legislature by the Basic Law—particularly in the area of political responsibility—were to combine with the electorate's acceptance of and the Social Democratic Party's (SPD) adaptation to the concept of the *Volkspartei* (a "catch-all" party as opposed to an ideological or special interest grouping) to make possible the emergence of effective parliamentary government and, at the same time, promote the idea of parties as instruments of government. Party influence was increased further by the weakness of the concept of an independent neutral sphere in German public life. There was no accepted doctrine of the limits of party. Interpretations of German historical experience tended to associate such doctrines with the reactionary predemocratic views of the *Obrigkeitsstaat,* a sovereign state with independent authority. Some of the peculiar qualities of West German parties derive in turn from the German tradition of legalism which is fortified by the Basic Law's commitment to the *Rechtsstaat* and its creation of the Federal Constitutional Court as the guarantor of that idea. Constitutional provisions are held (Leibholz, 1967) to confer a special legitimacy on the parties by creating a Parteienstaat. There are, however, problems of reconciling the Parteienstaat and the Rechtsstaat particularly apparent in the tension between the final authority of the Constitutional Court (such as, in determining what is a "constitutional" party) and party attempts to use the law as an instrument for political objectives. Since the early years of the Bonn republic, opposition parties have sought to use the "Road to Karlsruhe" to frustrate governments and obstruct the democratic decision of the legislature. The parties not only seek to influence appointments to the court through a system of *Proporz*, but they are also able to appeal to the court as final arbiter of cases which they lose in the legislative process. Such appeal is made easier by the right of a *Land* (state) government to take a case before it and by the provision for "abstract" judicial review. During the period after 1971 the cases of the Eastern treaties (where the court placed restrictions on future *Ostpolitik* negotiations) and of abortion law reform (rejected as unconstitutional) indicated the dangers of opposition abuse of the court. Indeed interparty negotiations about court appointments in 1971 were strongly influenced by the possibility of a future court decision on the Ostpolitik. Strengthening of the Rechtsstaat tradition did not therefore notably restrict party activity: the corollary of a strong Constitutional Court was party attempts to use it.

PARTY AND STATE IN WESTERN GERMANY

A theoretical controversy relating to the role of the political parties was sparked off by Leibholz's (1967) thesis of the "party state" (Parteienstaat). Professor Leibholz was a constitutional theorist as well as a prominent and long-serving member of the Federal Constitutional Court. As such he was able to exert considerable influence on its decisions. Despite its rudimentary nature the theory was also to have great influence in left-wing circles (Bermbach, 1970; Grebing, 1972). To Leibholz, Article 21 was the most significant feature of the new constitution; it legitimated the transition from the representative parliamentary system to "party state" democracy. The development of Volksparteien—the plebiscitary character of elections and the changed nature of executive-legislative relations—were to him further confirmation of the thesis. Parties encompass and mediate between state and society; they are quasi-state organs. They are "the surrogate of direct democracy in the modern territorial state," instruments of direct self-government by the people providing an "identity of will" between governors and governed. Parliament is simply a place where "instructed party delegates" meet to confirm decisions already arrived at in party committees or conferences. In other words the "democratic party state" had nothing in common with "liberal parliamentarianism."

Conservatives attacked the thesis for undermining the traditional autonomy of the executive power, whilst liberals like Hennis (1973) feared the Rousseauist democratic concepts upon which it was founded and the threat to the balance of public life when no limit is seen to the role of parties. The concept of direct democracy as applied to the parties threatened to strengthen them as democratic organs against the representative functions of the Bundestag. Moreover the confrontation of two "opposed" theses (liberal parliamentarianism and party democracy), which bear no relation to historical reality, asked the reader to make an unnecessary choice rather than analyse a complex reality. Leibholz presented a dogmatic construction of dubious opposites. The result was an ideological argument which bore no relation to historical facts or even to the sheer diversity of party structures in Western democracies. Therefore, it was not surprising to find him introducing qualifications which seemed to undermine his thesis, that is, the technical limits of direct democracy in the modern political system. Leibholz was attacked not only for the weaknesses of his thesis as a descriptive theory (for example, the parliamentary parties dominate party executives rather than vice-versa; the policy-making capacity of the parties vis-à-vis other institutions is limited; and the unity of action of the parties is over-estimated), but also for producing a normative theory which threatened the fundamentals of liberal democracy and served to discredit parliamentarianism as the earlier work of Carl Schmitt had done. Like Schmitt earlier and the "Frankfurt school" later (that is, Jürgen Habermas), he seemed to assume that representative government and "real" democracy are necessarily opposites. This common conviction reflected a factor of agreement between conservative anti-democratic and radical democratic thought.

The term Parteienstaat has in fact a significance which goes beyond Leibholz's exaggerated use of it. It tells us something about the hold which party elites have on the political system, about the degree to which (compared to Britain or France) the parties have permeated and enveloped other political elites. The all-pervasive role of parties contrasts with the failure of the Weimar parties to penetrate the centers of political power (Daalder, 1966: 60). In the Weimar Republic, traditionally powerful political elites tended either to participate in the party system with little commitment and reactionary intentions or they stayed outside altogether maintaining their influence through other power structures, notably the bureaucracy, the military, and the legal system. From 1945 the parties moved preemptively to forestall the rise of counter-elites by penetrating other institutions. Today party is established as the major channel of career advancement most notably in relation to the permanent bureaucracy. The key positions of political influence are to be obtained mainly through party channels. Party has become the major magnet for the ambitious, talented, and indeed opportunist individual. The traditional relationship between party and bureaucracy was profoundly upset by the legacy of the Third Reich and the circumstances of postwar occupation. Whatever restorative tendencies may have emerged within the bureaucracy — with the lack of impact of denazification and the traditional importance of public servants as politicians — the image of an objective impartial diviner of the "public interest" had received a bad blow. Reconstruction of the bureaucracy, even if on traditional lines, was guided by the party system.

This process of party "grip" on the political system was facilitated not just by the discrediting of historically prestigious institutions or by the aid of the occupation powers. The emergence of a stable party system and of the concept of a Volkspartei or "catch-all" party, with a broadly defined ideology serving to attract a maximum range of interests, combined to assist the process. In 1957 the CDU/CSU (the Christian Democratic Union and its Bavarian partner, the Christian Social Union) attained an absolute majority (although it continued to govern in coalition). By the mid 1960s commentators were talking of a "two-and-a-half" party system, whilst after 1969 a "two-block" party system seemed to have emerged (the Social Democrats and Free Democrats v. the Christian Democratic Union and the Christian Social Union). "Isolationist" parties like the Center Party, representing a particular subculture or interest, and "antisystem" parties like the Communists (till 1956 the KPD; after 1968 the DKP) were to prove of no real significance. Moreover the parties were to prove integrating agencies between political elites at national and local levels (Heidenheimer, 1958).

The quality of "stateness" in structural terms has been diffused in Western Germany. In the first place it joins party, parliament, government, and bureaucracy on novel terms. Whilst the bureaucracy may still appear (as in France) to remain the real location of distinct and autonomous state norms, the process of reconciliation between party and state means that it can no longer claim a monopoly. Parties are no longer solely concerned with representation or seen as divisive. Rather than simply pursuing an interest-based politics they have a strong moral function. The parties supply a high-level normative articulation through the political process, reducing the competition for norms. They are heirs to state norms, guardians of integration and *Ausgleich* on a higher plane than mere interest-based politics. One notes the strength of an intellectual and idealistic political vocabulary married to a moralizing and didactic style of political leadership. At the same time one must avoid identifying party and state. One major weakness of the concept of the Parteienstaat is that it assumes such an identification. The state is perhaps better understood as a sociocultural phenomenon rather than in terms of specific structures. There is a sense in which the state has been "dissolved" into society; it no longer possesses its traditional autonomy of society. It norms have been absorbed by diverse social, economic, and political actors whose attention is thereby directed to interdependency and the "whole" in significant ways. At the same time the state remains as an object of disaffection generating more structured "antisystem" movements than are to be found in Britain or the U.S. These movements remain insignificant compared to Weimar simply because responsibility norms and norms of belonging associated with the state are more widely diffused. Patterns of elite accommodation and the qualification of majoritarianism by a cooperative political style are therefore to be understood in terms of the state tradition rather than "consociational devices." [1]

THE IMPERATIVE MANDATE CONTROVERSY

Assimilation of the state tradition is a factor which has widened the gap between party leaderships and the apparatus on the one hand and the membership on the other. In the view of many critics (for example, Ellwein, 1973: 74) the former has taken on an excessive degree of autonomy vis-à-vis the membership. This problem was reflected from the late 1960s in the conflict within the SPD between militant advocates of internal party democracy and the party leadership. Controversy was sparked by the advocates of the imperative mandate particularly within the *Jusos* (Young Socialists). According to this doctrine parliamentarians were to be bound much more rigorously to party decisions and even removed from office (the recall) if their actions proved inconsistent with such decisions (Bermbach, 1970: 342). Individuals elected in the name of the party were to serve the party. Its supporters appealed to Article 21 GG and to Leibholz's view that Article 38—which guaranteed the parliamentarian's freedom of conscience and stressed his duty to represent the whole people—was a relic of an outworn conception of representation. To its critics (such as Trautmann, 1971) the imperative mandate reflected a theory of democracy which was wholly alien to the Basic Law (the identity principle as opposed to the representation principle). Article 38 serves to emphasize not only the separation of parliamentary party and extra-parliamentary party but also the rights of the individual within the parliamentary party. As such Article 38 can be seen as a precondition for internal party democracy. It could be argued in opposition to Leibholz that Articles 21 and 38 complemented rather than contradicted one another.

The controversy over the imperative mandate proved revealing. In reality there were comparatively few advocates of the doctrine in its strict sense; for example, Bermbach's (1970) controversial exposition of the imperative mandate was far from dogmatic. It is more accurate to speak of a general feeling amongst SPD party members that a more broadly based internal party discussion would be beneficial. Equally interesting was the behavior of SPD party leaders who tended to overreact to party claims for influence which by British standards were far from novel. Internal party interest in "programmatic politics" was interpreted as intervention in the processes of government. Identification with the state and its structures seemed to produce a distance between apparatus and membership in the parties so that parties appeared to take on a semi-autonomous existence. The concept of "state parties" is difficult to reconcile with ideas of internal party democracy. Despite warnings from the Constitutional Court in 1965 that the democratic process could only suffer from an overidentification of party and state, and despite commitments to internal party democracy in the Party Law of 1967, this process of identification has proved powerful. Whilst the Party Law produced large numbers of formal changes in party statutes, it was not followed by any substantial improvements in the practice of party democracy.

It was at the regional and local levels within the SPD that the issue was to prove important, particularly within the city-states of Hamburg and Bremen and the larger urban authorities like Frankfurt, Munich, and Hanover (Kaltefleiter and Veen, 1974). For example, in Munich the local party executive has sought with little success to subject the activities of the SPD in the city council to continuous and rigorous controls. As a consequence, relations between Lord Mayor Georg Kronawitter and the left-wing party leadership became notoriously bad. After the controversial case of Götz in 1973 (he was eventually refused appointment as a judge because of his membership of the German Communist Party), the SPD state executive committee in North-Rhine Westphalia decided that the Minister-President and SPD cabinet members must consult party organs before major decisions. The FDP coalition partner criticized this decision as the participation of party organs in government. Minister of the Interior Willi Weyer (FDP) threatened resignation in the same year over the claim by the SPD state party executive to a seat on the parliamentary coalition committee of SPD and FDP. The right of party organs to interfere in detailed issues was reflected even more dramatically in the increased frequency and length of state party conferences in Bremen and Hamburg, with consequent criticism that these city-state governments were dictated to by extra-parliamentary organs. There were seven special SPD party conferences in Hamburg in 1973, and copious resolutions were passed particularly with respect to specific industrial and transportation decisions. In 1973 the Hamburg SPD demanded that cabinet reshuffles be approved by conference; in 1974, following the election, three of the Lord Mayor's candidates for office were rejected by an extraordinary party congress. Following the entry of the FDP into coalition with the SPD in 1974, its state party congresses were to prove even more frequent than those of the SPD. The right of party organs to interfere in personnel decisions is perhaps best reflected in the famous case of Littmann, police chief of Frankfurt, whose replacement was demanded in 1970 by a party conference which had previously expressed displeasure at police policy concerning protest rallies. He was later to be replaced by the new Lord Mayor, Walter Möller (Bermbach, 1970). In September 1973 the local party organization decided that appointees to city office in Frankfurt would either be nominated by the party organization directly or need its assent (Kaltefleiter and Veen, 1974: 257). Already in the previous year it had successfully rejected attempts by the Lord Major Rudi Arndt to form a coalition with the FDP. Perhaps the most famous victory for the Left was in March 1972, when the Bremen SPD party congress decided on a separation of party office and elected mandate. It was argued by the Left in Bremen that accumulation of office and mandate produced an oligopoly of power and excessive conservatism in leadership. Their opponents feared that such creative tension would degenerate into loss of effective governmental leadership as members of the *Senat* were deprived of influence within the party.

There has been a tendency in German academic and political debate on these events to exaggerate their significance, and indeed by 1976 the issue of the imperative mandate had largely subsided. Their consequences are largely dictated by the strength of political leadership locally and regionally. For example, whilst Peter Schulz as Lord Mayor of Hamburg had great difficulty coping with internal party pressures, his successor Ulrich Klose displayed much greater skills in this respect. The political ascendancy of Hans Koschnick in Bremen has not been displaced by the new activism in the SPD there. Extra-parliamentary party organizations have been notably lacking in success in their attempts to impose their views on parliamentary parties. Much of the controversy is the product of opposing two ideal-types, the free mandate and the imperative mandate, neither of which exists or is likely to exist in its pure form. Whereas Article 38 is more important for its existence than for its strict application, enforcement of the imperative mandate is limited by the continuing discretion enjoyed by elected members. Even though the imperative mandate is not provided for in the Basic Law, these two principles of political responsibility coexist, and the politician must maneuver with skill in the grey zone between them. Cooperation and tension will continue to characterize the relations between parliamentary and extra-parliamentary parties. The pressure to shift the balance in favour of greater intraparty control is a consequence of the view that present representative forms are inadequate in a modern industrialized society with increasing governmental intervention and with an educated population who increasingly recognize the effect of governmental decisions on their lives and seek to influence these decisions. It represents an interest in "programmatic" politics and broader policy discussions which is not altogether unwelcome in the Federal Republic.

The debate concerning the imperative mandate reflects above all different conceptions of the role of parties in the political process. Party leaderships see a danger of a return to traditional concepts of party in Germany with consequences for political stability. Their supporters see a threat from the Left of a return to traditional concepts of direct democracy which threaten representative forms. They fear that parties will be reduced to ideological forums or mere pressure groups. As instruments of government, parties need to be flexible rather than dogmatic. Instead the imperative mandate threatens to introduce a new dogmatism, a loss of attention to the middle ground, and an emphasis on intraparty problems rather than on interparty collaboration and competition. Coalition government necessitates a wide discretion for party leaders to negotiate anyway. There are also fears of a loss of continuity, effectiveness, and clear responsibility as issues are decided in the anonymity of party organs. Most of all the imperative mandate threatens to replace the authority of the voter by the rule of party delegates. Only some 4 percent of voters are members of parties and of these only about 30 percent could be labelled activists. Broad-based democracy—attention to a wide range of public views—is therefore likely to be lost in favour of government by an elite of party activists. Moreover, the important practical problem of which party organs are to have the right to deprive the parliamentarian of his independence is not clearly solved—constituency parties, regional or state party congresses, federal party congresses, or some mixture of these. The answer is crucial to internal party power structure. Whatever the answer to this question, in the end effective government will depend on striking a balance between opposing principles. However, in West Germany such a balance is difficult to achieve because of the nature of German constitutionalism. The problem of the imperative mandate reflects a widespread tendency in German politics to assert a discrepancy between norm and reality, *Verfassung* and *Verfassungswirklichkeit,* as the basis for political criticism—in other words to pose the problem of constitutionalism in an extreme form (Hennis,

1968). Supporters of both Articles 21 and 38 assert such a discrepancy, condemn political reality accordingly, or assert the need for constitutional revision. Mutual accommodation is as a result very difficult.

ABUSE OF THE BUNDESRAT?

The SPD was not the only party which could be said to present the danger of an excessive extension of the influence of party within the political system. Control over the Bundesrat (the upper house) has always been a sensitive political question because this institution has the right of absolute veto over matters affecting the administrative, financial, and territorial interests of the states. Consequently, most domestic policy legislation is subject to its agreement. During the seventh Bundestag (1972-1976), the debate concerning whether the CDU/CSU was using its one-vote majority in the Bundesrat to blockade the SPD/FDP government's program reached a climax. After this majority was increased to eleven votes in early 1976, the question of whether it was possible to govern against the wishes of the CDU/CSU was posed even more dramatically.[2] The Bundesrat is an unusual federal organ which can only be understood in terms of German constitutional and political history. Its membership is made up from state governments who, as compensation for having to execute most federal laws, are permitted to participate in their formulation through this organ. As a consequence of generous interpretations of its authority and the growing legislative competence of the federation, it has become an increasingly powerful institution. Traditionally it has been criticized for its excessive bureaucratization as state officials in the Bundesrat committees reduced political questions to administrative issues (Merkl, 1959).

Its background role was however to disappear quickly after 1969. Chancellor Brandt was soon to refer to it as a *Neinsage-Maschine,* and various SPD politicians were to speak of the dangers of a "countergovernment" (Schindler, 1974). It was felt that the Bundesrat was being used not just as an "extended arm" of the Bundestag opposition but even as a means of opposition participation in the process of government. There were fears that if it became a second political battlefield the whole federal order might be endangered. The CDU/CSU was thought to be unable to recognize limits to its opposition role in its search to regain power at the federal level. It was accused of behaving like a government in exile. SPD anxieties were reinforced by setbacks in state elections, the emergence of critical domestic problems after 1973, and by the slow progress of domestic reforms. It was possible, therefore, for the CDU/CSU to argue that the Bonn coalition was seeking a scapegoat for its own failure. In August 1974 the

Federal Constitutional Court produced a much disputed judgment (on the issue of whether Bundesrat approval was necessary for the fourth amendment to the *Rentenversicherungsgesetz*, the pension insurance law) which in narrowing down some Bundesrat claims to competence made comments concerning the role of the Bundesrat which were interpreted as criticism of the CUD/CSU strategy of using it as an important instrument of opposition. However, this badly worded judgment did nothing to resolve the different interpretations of the functions and reality of operations of the Bundesrat produced by the political parties.

The answer to the question of whether the CDU/CSU has been abusing the Bundesrat depends on one's views about the purposes of the institution (for the views outlined in this paragraph see Scheuing, 1974). Here two major issues arise. First, some commentators such as Theodor Maunz argue that the Parliamentary Council's clear rejection of the Senate principle in favour of the traditional German Council principle implies that its sole function is to represent the interests of the states and to bring administrative expertise to bear on issues. Hence its use by a party to oppose the federal government is unconstitutional. On this basis prominent SPD politicians have argued that since 1969 party political calculation has been taking precedence over *Sachlichkeit* (objectivity, realism) and *Sachbezogenheit* (relevance), thereby abusing the Bundesrat. By contrast, Gerhard Leibholz and Theodor Eschenburg point out that since Bundesrat membership is drawn from state governments this implies acceptance of its party political role too. Oppositions can be expected to use whatever instruments are available to attain influence on political development. Indeed in the past the SPD had not been averse to adopting party political stances in the Bundesrat. In 1956, for example, Adenauer had expressed anxieties about its "party dependency." West Germany is a party state as well as a federal state; the *Bundesstaatsprinzip* of Article 20 (i) is overlaid by the *Parteienstaatsprinzip* of Article 21 (i). The consequences are twofold. Federal and state politics are seen by the political parties in terms of an integrated and comprehensive strategy. The Bundesrat probably offers to the opposition a more important method to control the federal government and to formulate alternatives than the Bundestag. Hence federal party organizations seek to coordinate party organizations in the states, to conduct state elections in terms of federal issues, and to conduct the formation of state governments from the perspective of the distribution of seats in the Bundesrat. Moreover, there emerges a dual democratically legitimate federal majority rather than a single majority parliamentary system on British lines. With opposed majorities since 1969 the party political element in the Bundesrat emerges more clearly. It is therefore doubtful that the use of the Bundesrat as an instrument of opposition is unconstitutional. Nevertheless, its members appear to have a clear conception that it is not there simply to oppose but to synthesize *Sachlichkeit* (objectivity, impartiality, realism) and party politics. There seems to be widespread agreement that "obstructive" opposition would constitute "misuse."

There is a further controversy about the nature of the Bundesrat. To some it is essentially a second chamber, indeed a "super" second chamber because of its important veto power. In fact the Constitutional Court in its judgment of 1974 rejected the view that it was a second chamber; it was merely to "assist" in the federal legislative process. Others argue that the Bundesrat is essentially an "auxiliary government" (*Nebenregierung*) as a consequence of its composition (state ministers) and its preoccupation with administrative questions. This dispute relates primarily to the problem that there is no overall concept like Parliament or Congress which incorporates two chambers in Western Germany. Despite the judgment of the Constitutional Court it is better seen as a special type of second chamber which is not strictly part of parliament. Like the Bundestag and the federal government, it is a federal organ concerned with general issues of policy and serving the interests of the states and of the federal system. As such its opposition to major decisions is not necessarily a misuse.

An opposition strategy was handicapped by coalition arrangements after 1969 and only emerged as state elections led to the end of CDU/FDP (that is, Rhineland-Palatinate) and SPD/CDU (that is, Lower Saxony, Baden-Würtemberg) coalitions in the states. As each state delivers a bloc vote in the Bundesrat, these coalitions were faced by serious internal problems with the coalition partner which participated in the federal government either insisting on withdrawal of the Bundesrat vote or threatening to end the state coalition government prematurely (as happened in Lower Saxony in 1970). The development of a two-group party system, SPD/FDP vs. CDU/CSU, and one party CDU governments in the states of Rhineland-Palatinate, Baden-Würtemberg, and Schleswig-Holstein were the real precondition for the dual-majority problem. A stragegy of opposition was only possible when state governments to which the opposition partner belonged were constituted only from the opposition parties. Developments in the party system have then been of major significance to the evolution of the Bundesrat's role. The post-1969 situation offered a new opportunities for political profile in the Bundesrat and encouraged threats of absolute veto on a new scale. Consequent political interest in the Bundesrat had effects on its style with livelier plenary sessions characterized by polemical interruptions (Laufer, 1970: 318). It became increasingly an organ of CDU/CSU party publicity and prolonged opposition with politicians like Hans Filbinger and Franz Heubl using its plenary sessions to state party principle. According to Heubl it had awoken from its long political sleep. In this context Bavaria emerged as a new source of initiative for bills. SPD politicians responded by suggestions that West Berlin be given full voting rights and that populous states like North-Rhine Westphalia deserved more votes (Schindler, 1974). The federal government (SPD/FDP) increased the number of "urgent government proposals" under Article 26 (2) of the Basic Law; in such cases the Bundesrat has only three weeks to respond.[3] Increased use was made of the possibility of introducing government bills into the Bundestag as bills of the parliamentary parties at the same time as they were submitted to the Bundesrat, thereby eliminating the need for the government to wait for Bundesrat views before submitting proposals to the Bundestag. It was therefore argued in response by the the CDU/CSU that the federal government was misusing its right of initiative, threatening proper Bundesrat consideration of proposals and undermining traditional norms or cooperation.

SPD/FDP irritation could not really be directed at the number of government bills rejected by the Bundesrat (only one in the period 1969-1974 compared to three in the period 1961-1965) but rather at the motives underlying the threats expressed by CDU/CSU state government representatives. Certainly its very full and ambitious program had to suffer considerable delays; frustration was increased by the number of major compromises which it felt compelled to make.[4] There were even cases of CDU officials being left in sensitive administrative positions in Bonn in order to facilitate passage of major legislation through the Bundesrat. In issues like divorce law reform the government took account of CDU/CSU views at the drafting stage, anticipating political difficulties. Government attempts to introduce speed restrictions on autobahns were frustrated in the Bundesrat. Different drafts of a higher education framework bill were rejected as unnecessary by the CDU/CSU states in the Bundesrat, whilst an increase of turnover tax as a major component of economic policy in 1975 was also blocked. Despite verbal threats from politicians like ex-Chancellor Kurt Georg Kiesinger, Minister-President Hans Filbinger, and Bavarian Minister for Federal Affairs Franz Heubl, the CDU/CSU displayed recognition of the dangers of overuse of the Bundesrat for the purpose of opposition.[5] In fact in 1970 the Bundesrat nominated SPD candidates to the Constitutional Court unanimously. Whilst the behavior of the CDU/CSU state governments was shaped by party political concepts and electoral tactics as well as state interests, there was willingness to back down in the arbitration committee composed of Bundestag and Bundesrat members where the government had a majority anyway until early 1976. There was no more resort to the arbitration committee than usual; the major difference was the number of sensitive bills involved. In other words politicization of the Bundesrat has not been at the expense of political wisdom. Respect for precedence has tempered exhaustive use of constitutional possibilities; political formalism has given way to "good sense." The Bundesrat has preferred in this way to protect its privileged access to information. Maintenance of the convention of courtesy which governs the federal government's release of information to the Bundesrat gives its members a privileged access to government, enables smooth working of the Bundesrat committees, and places restraints on its opposition role. The executive and bureaucratic elements within it continue therefore to prevent its complete politicization.

One factor which has hindered an effective opposition strategy through the Bundesrat has been the very complex political decision-making process which underlies its work. The major decisions about how to vote are taken *outside* the institution. Usually such decisions are taken in separate state cabinets with references to particular state interests and party rivalries. Representatives of state governments are rarely given discretion to negotiate their bloc vote. For particularly controversial decisions—such as the ratification of the Polish Treaty in 1976 and earlier of the non-aggression treaty with the U.S.S.R. and the treaty on the limitation of nuclear weapons—coordination takes place through ad hoc meetings of the minister-presidents of the same party, and federal governments have always sought to coordinate "their" state governments which thus gain privileged information. Although as a consequence coordination has traditionally been better between CDU/CSU states, the relations between state governments, the Bundestag party leadership, and national party leadership continue to be difficult. Therefore, coordination of party positions in the Bundesrat remains poor (Laufer, 1970).

The greater party politicization of the Bundesrat has had two important effects:

(1) The institution has been subjected to increased public attention, particularly by the media, and its political significance has been better recognized; it can be argued that its activities have been democratized and its tendency to "bureaucratic autonomy" has been counteracted.

(2) There has been a growing tendency to view state elections as "Bundesrat elections" (when there is a possibility of a change in power at the state level) or as "correctives" to the previous federal election; in other words, one function of the Bundesrat is to mirror public opinion as expressed in state elections to the federal government.

State election results influence the legislative climate in Bonn not only by their effects on the morale of the federal government, but also because of their effects on the opposition in the Bundesrat. The key examples of "Bundesrat elections" in the seventh Bundestag were Lower Saxony (summer 1974) and North-Rhine Westphalia (spring 1975) where the possibility of an increased CDU majority in the Bundesrat had a decisive effect on the themes, style, and personalities involved in the campaign. The Bundesrat is then inevitably a party-political insititution; at the same it is much more.

German politicians must live with the fact that the principle of government by parliamentary majority is qualified in the Federal Republic by the existence of a dual majority at the federal level. This problem contributes to and is in turn exacerbated by a lack of clarity concerning the role of opposition in the Federal Republic. There has been a danger that oppositions might behave as if they were a "government in exile" or counter-government instead of concentrating on providing an alternative government. Whilst this was apparent in the SPD just after 1949, it became a much more serious threat after 1969 and placed great demands on the political wisdom and self-restraint of politicians.

THE "PARTY BOOK" ADMINISTRATION

Much of the character of West German politics and administration is shaped by the existence of an extensive twilight zone where politics and administration converge. There is no clear demarcation in terms of career patterns and styles between politics and administration and no conception of politically neutral policy advice at the center of government. Whilst such a phenomenon is not new to students of American or French government, in Western Germany this twilight zone takes on a peculiar form and has distinctive consequences for the political system. It lends an administrative style to German politics and produces a widespread dissemination of respect for official expertise and technical competence. At the same time there is the absence of a bureaucratic elite on French lines, self-confident of its ability to divine a higher-order public interest transcending current politics. The German bureaucracy emerged weakened and discredited from the Third Reich: its claims to stand above or beyond politics seemed no longer credible. Despite continuity of machinery, methods, and (until the late 1960s) personnel, the fundamental role conceptions of the German administrator have undergone drastic alteration (Putnam, 1973). The chief agency of this transformation has been the political parties whose ascendancy has produced a permeation of administrative institutions by external interests. This process of permeation (*Verfilzung*) and its consequences for government and administration have become an increasingly controversial theme in recent years.

Many of the political problems associated with the public service stem from the highly developed, perhaps overdeveloped, concept of the civil service. Public officials (*Beamte, Angestellte, Arbeiter*) are to be found at all levels of government and in all public law institutions.[6] Their presence defines the scope of the state. The sheer size of the German public service and the fact that it includes such groups as university professors, teachers, railway and post personnel make it difficult to avoid its party politicization. So many diverse groups are drawn into the net of official duties as well as rights and are a major reason why the problem of radicals is sensitive and difficult to resolve.[7] Bonn's public service laws ensure that German officials (*Beamte*) are not deprived of the right to be active in party work or to pursue a parliamentary career. Officials who are elected to parliament (federal or state) are permitted to go on paid leave for two months during the election campaign, continue to receive a sizeable proportion of their official salary as well as their parliamentary allowance, and do not lose their claim to pension rights. They are in other words a privileged political group whose "expert" background and financial security assist their advance within the political parties. Apologists for these privileges stress the political independence of officials in elected assemblies. Unlike in Britain a civil service career is not an alternative to a political career; it may even be a preferred route into a political career. These political privileges of the official are in fact difficult to remove as a result of the presence of large bodies of officials in parliaments and their dominance in the parliamentary interior committees that deal with public service affairs. The proportion of parliamentarians who are officials has always been high in German history. They emerged in nineteenth-century parliaments as something of a substitute political class for an assertive independent bourgeoisie on British or French lines. There they formed a basis for generally cooperative relations between parliaments and executives and were to continue as a considerable force despite the competition of rising economic interests. A combination of high intellectual and personal qualities, sheer legal and technical competence, and independent authority assured them a strong place. They accounted for some 52 percent of the National Assembly in 1848, 47 percent of the Prussian Assembly of the 1860s, and 22 percent of the Reichstag in 1907 (Hess, 1976).

Public service law also recognizes the existence of "political" officials who can be removed at the discretion of the minister. Examples of such officials include state secretaries and heads of divisions at the federal level. Their existence has a "demonstration" effect on the public service; the ambitious official at a lower level is encouraged to join the "right" political party or at least to make his sympathies known if he wishes to rise to the top. Hence extra-administrative factors are recognized by officials themselves to play an important part in appointments and promotions (Senatskanzlei Bremen, 1972). Of course no career system is ever strictly mechanical in the sense of being based solely on technical criteria; sociopolitical evaluations enter into the process. However, in the Federal Republic such evaluations are not simply based on internal administrative criteria of social cohesion and political integrity and neutrality. Career judgments are more frequently permeated by party political considerations.[8] Such a practice can of course be justified by reference to the deep involvement of officials in the preparation of government reforms, the importance of their discretionary decisions to government strategy, and the difficulties which ministers and cabinets have in appraising administrative proposals. Once again the class of "political" officials goes back into German tradition. The Imperial public service law of 1873 introduced a much larger class which was extended still further by a law of 1907.

Germany has in fact a long history of "negative" party patronage with respect to the public service in order to weed out potential "unreliables." Such "unreliables" have included Catholics and Social Democrats in the Bismarck period; Jews, "communists," and "Weimar appointees" in the Third Reich; those who suffered from denazification in the late 1940s, and left-wing radicals in the 1970s (Dyson, 1975a). More active forms of party patronage were practiced during the Weimar period particularly in the Prussian administration (including the judiciary) and in local government. However, the "Weimar appointees" did not form a homogenous group, were assimilated within the public service fairly easily, and failed to offset the traditional nepotism of right-wing student corporations (Eschenburg, 1974: 76). The loyalty of the supposedly apolitical and neutral public bureaucracy was never effectively secured by the Weimar Republic. This historical legacy was to have a major effect on attitudes towards the bureaucracy in the Bonn Republic.

After 1945 the relatively unsuccessful attempt at denazification of the public service was complemented by the high point of active party patronage. The parties emerged undisputably as the most "reliable" institutions with the full support of the Allies. Membership in a licensed party was the most tangible sign of democratic reliability for candidates for the public service. From a general point of view, and with the Weimar experience in mind, regime loyalty was best guaranteed by party members in the bureaucracy. Party patronage had, however, other functions (Eschenburg,

1961), including a welfare function. With the end of the Second World War, Germany took on many of the characteristics of a "melting-pot" society; parties could offer material services to refugees and "displaced" persons. Public service employment for Catholics and for Social Democrats could be justified as compensation for Nazi persecution. As a consequence a rivalry concerning appointments and promotions broke out between the SPD on the one hand and the Catholic Church and the CDU/CSU on the other. The patronage of one evoked the patronage of the other. Out of this rivalry developed an interest in *Proporz* patronage, witnessed most clearly in local government. Perhaps the clearest form of such patronage was practiced by BHE (the Block of Expellees and Refugees) ministers in federal and many state coalition governments; as Ministers for Refugee Affairs they were to assist not only refugees but also many "displaced" ex-Nazis (Eschenburg, 1974: 80). Patronage is still used by the parties either as a reward for good party work or as a method of "buying off" political opposition within the party. In either case the more active party workers are involved. This form of patronage is, however, typically confined to lower levels. At higher levels it takes the form of appointment to the supervisory boards of public law or state undertakings in, for example, banking or transport. A second form of patronage is *Herrschaftspatronage,* an attempt to extend party control by placing party members in key positions in administration. This practice may be used by an individual minister to control his department or by his party to restrain or control the minister.

Patronage was therefore a complex and difficult phenomenon because of the various motives guiding it. Moreover party patronage became intertwined with "religious patronage" (furthered by the close links between the Catholic Church and the CDU) and "interest group patronage" (also facilitated by links between interest groups and political parties). Farming organizations, trade unions, professional and industrial associations sought to place reliable men in the ministries of key importance to them, and the parties for whom support of major interests was essential were only too willing to oblige. By 1947 the Allies were already seeking to reduce the extent of patronage by insisting on strict implementation of the career service principle and by reducing the political rights and privileges of officials. These two Allied ideas were enforced on the Bizonal Economic Council, but despite Allied wishes were not adopted by the new federal government after 1949. The bureaucrats resented any diminution of their political rights and their presence in the Parliamentary Council and in the Bundestag after 1949 precluded any such reform. Party hostility to the Allied proposals was governed by the scarcity of able and reliable parliamentarians; the expertise of officials was felt to be needed in parliament. The SPD also feared that depoliticization would lead to the resurrection of the view that the public service stood "above" party. Reestablishment of the traditional career principle in the public service law was not, therefore, combined with depoliticization of the public service.

During the early years of the new republic two factors had in fact worked against party politicization of the Bonn bureaucracy:

(1) The Central Personnel Office of the Bizonal Council had appointed many SPD officials as a result of its "neutral" personnel policy; many of these officials later got jobs in Bonn.

(2) Adenauer and his State Secretary in the Chancellery, Hans Globke, favored the career principle and sought with some success to build an administrative elite unattached to party; during the period of CDU dominance there was in fact no tradition of filling all "political" posts in the bureaucracy with party members.

Nevertheless, decentralized personnel management permitted individual ministries to pursue patronage at the expense of further appointment and promotion of SPD officials. Typically ministers displayed considerable interest in personnel policy. There was of course great variation depending on the conceptions of individual ministers and their senior civil servants. In the early years there was a close relationship (approved by Globke) between the Catholic student corporation CV and federal ministries. Of even greater significance during the years of CDU dominance in Bonn was the colonization within certain ministries of the central administrative divisions dealing with personnel, budgetary, and organizational questions by CDU members or sympathizers. After the change of power in 1969, lack of SPD control over these divisions was to be a source of considerable irritation.

Two major changes were to combine from the mid 1960s to illustrate the degree of party politicization of administration at all levels. SPD participation in the federal government after 1966 and its ascendancy after 1969 coincided with a period of retirement of the first postwar administrative generation and the impact of demographic changes produced by the Second World War. Posts were gradually filled by a new postwar generation whose administrative role conception was much more politically conscious in nature and whose rapid advancement was assisted by the so-called "missing generation." The close involvement of such officials in party thinking and decisions was distrusted in many sectors of the administration—particularly the Interior and Finance Ministries where traditional values of political detachment and neutrality were still strong. However, in other sectors the CDU had already been drawing officials into essentially party work. In fact its ability to use the federal bureaucracy had been one reason why the CDU had failed to build up its own party organization as the SPD had done. Lack of governmental change had encouraged an uncritical identification and over-engagement of some officials, and there were cases of CDU/CSU misuse of officials. For example, higher officials were active in CDU/CSU parliamentary party meetings, and *Beamte* were sometimes used for highly party political functions in some ministries, for example as aides in election campaigns.

It is, however, very difficult to measure the extent of political appointments particularly as officials can be rotated between posts ostensibly on administrative grounds but in reality for party political purposes. Over 70 reposting were made, for example, in October-November 1969 although not in every case on political grounds. Earlier factionalism within the CDU had led to personnel changes particularly in the Chancellery on the succession of Adenauer by Erhard and of Erhard by Kiesinger. In 1969 only 16 of the 66 higher officials in the Chancellery were CDU/CSU members, although the number of "sympathists" was clearly higher. Horst Ehmke's view as head of the Chancellery was that a strategy of preventive action was better than the risks of a strategy of cooperation. The SPD was to make wholesale replacements of "political" officials stretching down to below division leader level in the Chancellor's office (Dyson, 1974). Whilst commentators spoke of Horst Ehmke "running amock with a machine gun" in the Chancellery, Alex Möller at the Ministry of Finance was accused of a "blood bath." Both State Secretaries (Grund and Hettlage) in the Finance Ministry had been closely involved in Franz Josef Strauss's election campaign; they and four out of seven division heads were removed. Strangely, of all the officials removed in the Finance Ministry only one was not reemployed there. Eleven State Secretaries and eight heads of divisions were replaced immediately in 1969. There was not only a growing tendency to appoint party members to "political" posts but also an increasing use in these positions of "irregulars" drawn from outside the federal service. Helmut Schmidt, first as Minister of Defence and after 1972 as Finance and Economics Minister, was fond of bringing in outside talent. Under his successor, Finance Minister Hans Apel, top "political" posts were increasingly staffed by such "irregulars." [9] Faced by a bureaucracy whose responsiveness was distrusted, SPD ministers employed a variety of techniques. For example, in many ministries there was wholesale rotation of "distrusted" individuals from key positions to marginal ones; as new posts were often created for this purpose, this procedure was to prove expensive.[10] Below the "political" posts there was in some ministries an interest in appointing and promoting SPD officials. Finally, attempts were made to bypass or complement the work of existing divisions or bureaus (*Referate*) by setting up new units, such as planning units staffed by party sympathizers. Considerable tension was often generated by these practices between "star" SPD officials and those who had been bypassed. The porous nature of the administration, its proneness to leaks and revelations, was further reinforced. This politicization of the administration—which had not been begun by the SPD but had been seriously reinforced by them—underlined the lack of an esprit de corps in Bonn at administrative levels. Integration of government and even within ministries was implicitly regarded as a political as well as a technical administrative problem (Dyson, 1975c).

The political coloring of Bonn ministries is partly a product of ministerial views and partly a product of self-selection by officials. Both these factors combined before 1969 to produce both trade union and left-wing CDU influence in the Ministry of Labor and Social Affairs, whilst FDP as well as CDU influence was apparent in the ministries of Economics and Finance. For similar reasons the most spectacular case of SPD dominance is the Development Ministry. Under Minister Erhard Eppler there developed within this ministry the "Monday Group," composed of leftists who produced progressive proposals outside the normal hierarchy. Individual ministries have witnessed changes of emphasis over time. Whereas Georg Leber pursued a largely neutral personnel policy at the Minstry of Transport, his successors have attempted more active patronage policies, including "irregulars," with consequences for the climate of internal relations. Problems of internal party control combined with the colonization of different divisions by different transportation interests to make the Transport Ministry a classic case of poor coordination. At the Justice Ministry after 1969 Gerhard Jahn pushed through SPD appointments and promotions; by contrast Hans-Jochen Vogel has pursued a neutral policy. FDP ministers at the Foreign Ministry and the Interior Ministry have pursued the most neutral personnel policies, whilst Hans Friderichs (FDP and formerly a state secretary in the CDU government of Rhineland-Palatinate) as Economics Minister has surrounded himself with CDU sympathizers including one of his state secretaries.

The adaptive capacity of the administrative system to these changes should not be underestimated. Various attempts were made to establish special bodies to watch over the "CDU bureaucracy." For example, in certain ministries planners with highly specific and special functions were appointed directly responsible to the minister or state secretary. Karl Schiller as Minister of Economics (later of Economics and Finance) and his successor Helmut Schmidt appointed "invisible planners" in the form of special personal groups outside the normal organization structure. They operated in a quiet but occasionally influential manner to offset internal friction and avoid the political limelight. In the Economics Ministry they succeeded along with the *Grundsatzabteilung* (central policy division) in establishing (secretly) a concept of six- to nine-month forward planning. There were, however, numerous important issues, such as the law against restriction of competition, where they failed to achieve influence. In this case Wolfgang Kartte (CDU), head of the competition section in the ministry, Otto Schlecht, head of the Grundsatzabteilung and former personal assistant to Erhard's state secretary, Interior Minister Hans-Dietrich Genscher (FDP) through his Working Group on Domestic Policy, the CDU opposition, and industrial associations were to prove far more powerful than SPD party perspectives (Grottian, 1974). More formal staff line constructions for planning to introduce greater concern for overall political strategy were to prove even more abortive, generating conflicts of competence as well as conflicts over substantive issues. From mid-1970 planning units and project groups lost their significance (for example, those in the Chancellery) or were abolished. An earlier example of this tendency was the Labor Ministry where in 1968 the somewhat isolated planning staff advising Walter Arendt was integrated into a reformed Grundsatzabteilung. Indeed strengthening of the Grundsatzabteilung (for example, in the Economics Ministry) seemed to provide a more secure foundation for less ambitious planning efforts, whilst existing ministry divisions responded to the threat of new planning developments by reinforcing their own planning capacity. Such adaptive mechanisms ensured that the balance of power within ministries altered little.

Even where SPD personnel policies have been most actively pursued SPD domination is far from complete. The central administrative divisions of both the Federal Chancellor's Office and the Federal Press and Information Office remain strongly conservative. At present only two out of five division heads in the Chancellery are SPD members. One consequence of party politicization was a deterioration in the quality of personal relations which, for example, made difficult the work of the Chancellery's two successive central planners, Professor Reimut Jochimsen and Albrecht Müller. Chancellery Minister Ehmke's personnel policies after 1969 were to come into conflict with the CDU-dominated Personnel Council (*Personalrat*) of the Chancellery; its chairman, whilst still a Chancellery official, was to publish a bitter attack on the consequences (including the Guillaume affair) of this personnel policy (Seeman, 1975). The limited system of codetermination practiced in ministries through the Personalräte was to illuminate the extent of party politicization and reinforce internal interest in the politics of personnel. For example, in 1971 the Personalrat of the Federal Ministry for Youth, Family, and Health publicized its opposition to party promotion of officials at the expense of merit. Internal personnel politics can be quite severe with frequent cases of conflict over appointments and promotions between the majority on the Personalrat and ministers, for example in the Federal Press and Information Office. Where senior officials are appointed against the advice of the Personalrat (such as Claus Noé in the Economics Ministry) internal bureaucratic support for that individual later remains problematic. Union representatives on these councils frequently adopt the case of aggrieved party members; the ÖTV (Federation of Public Servants and Transport Workers Union) typically defends the SPD whilst the DBB (*Deutscher Beamtenbund*) supports the CDU.

Traditionally the German official (*Beamte*) is supposed to be in a special relationship of service and trust to the state, embodying the "objective justice and order" of the state above the parties and parliament. This relationship is still spelled out in the details of the public service laws and reflected in the special ethos of the career public service with its characteristics of homogeneity, unity, social prestige, and caste consciousness (Ellwein and Zoll, 1973: 22). The career principle, special training and service provisions, and the principle of "party political neutrality" reinforce its special ethos and status. It is not surprising then if democratic reformers have in the 1950s and 1960s expressed anxieties about the degree of continuity in the public service (Eschenburg, 1974: 90). And yet despite the heritage of tradition apparent in Article 33 of the Basic Law and the public service laws (Ellwein, 1973: 370-374) and the difficulties of reform of *Beamtentum,* a new type of Beamte has clearly emerged—one who is better able to cope with the new demands occasioned by the changed functions of the administration within the political system. In the context of the "active" public service state involved in new functions of political planning the official is drawn much more closely into political issues as an adviser on policy options, negotiator with interests, and decision maker who often has considerable discretion at his disposal. It is clear that the informational advantages of the public service over other institutions enable it to develop its own powerful ideas and alternatives. The concept of a policy innovation function for the administrator along with an "internal engagement" for political values is bound up with the function of long-term political planning (Steinkemper, 1974: 11). Consequently greater problems of political direction and control arise. There is a potential threat to the Parteienstaat.

Empirical research on senior officials has in fact revealed that this threat has been counteracted by increased party use of the institution of the *politische Beamte* ("political" officials) to exert greater political direction and to introduce new characteristics into the public service which in themselves constitute a major reform. Although the "change in power" in 1969 did not constitute a personnel revolution, there is strong evidence of a "silent" revolution since the mid-1960s affecting CDU as well as SPD governments. Whilst the Fulton Report in Britain (1968) may have occasioned more apparent reform activity than the Report of the Study Commission for the Reform of Public Service Law in the Federal Republic (1973), the British reforms have proved much less significant. Parties as reform-agents in the Federal Republic have brought about much more impoliticization and a more positive role conception are even apparent below the level of "political" officials. Both amongst the "political" officials (state secretaries at federal and state levels and also division heads at the federal level and amongst senior "nonpolitical" officials [subdivision heads at the federal level and division heads at the state level]) there is emerging a new type of politically conscious official who is less detached and procedure-oriented and more problem-and-program-oriented, more open and flexible for new problem-solving strategies (Putnam, 1973; Steinkemper, 1974). Provisions in public service law regarding the need for discretion in personal political activity and "neutrality" (*Uberparteilichkeit*) no longer reflect reality (if they ever did). The higher public service as defined above (in terms of "political" and "nonpolitical" officials) has undergone enormous changes in age structure, career backgrounds, strength of party identification, and degree of integration with the rest of society. As a consequence the pictures offered by Armstrong (1973: 181), Ellwein and Zoll (1973), Johnson (1968: 148) and Wildenmann (1968) have been rapidly outdated. Putnam's (1973) and Steinkemper's (1974) surveys undertaken in 1970 and 1972 respectively offer a new picture. The value of the Steinkemper study is further enhanced by the fact that it is part of a more general survey of leadership groups.[13]

In terms of the number of different previous outside jobs occupied, the Steinkemper study indicated that senior officials (as defined above) were only surpassed by political and trade union leaders. Thus, 23 percent of senior officials interviewed had very heterogenous career experiences (that is, in three or more sectors), 69 percent had been active in two or more sectors, and 8 percent (14.5 percent of "political" officials interviewed) were in their first public service post. Only one-third of those interviewed had had exclusively public service careers (Steinkemper, 1974: 22-30). *Aussenseiter* (outsiders) have clearly become a major phenomenon in the higher public service. Their careers do not follow public service rules strictly, and therefore they are likely to be oriented more to outside reference groups than to internal administrative norms. At senior levels there was a very high representation of officials with practical experience in economic and industrial organizations, most notably in economics and finance ministries and other ministries with economic functions (such as transport, agriculture, labor). In these ministries at the federal level the proportion of such officials at senior levels exceeded one-third. In other ministries at the federal level officials with a background in economic and industrial affairs accounted for just under 16 percent of senior officials (Steinkemper, 1974: 27). An even higher proportion were drawn from the world of education and research. Not surprisingly there was a concentration in education ministries (38.5 percent in state education ministries); however, the average for federal ministries was over 21 percent. Of great interest was the large proportion previously active in politics, whether as elected representatives or party officials at different levels of the political system. At the federal level just over 15 percent of "political" officials (30.8 percent of state secretaries) had had political careers; the proportion amongst state secretaries at the *Land* level was over 21 percent (Steinkemper, 1974: 26). Movement was not, however, simply one way. The public service itself provides a "reservoir of personnel" for higher education, banking, and industry. Over 9 percent of the economic elite and over 8 percent of the scholars (*Wissenschaftler*) were recruited from people whose careers had begun in the public service (Steinkemper, 1974: 25). Just over 27 percent of senior politicians interviewed had spent part of their career in the public service; over 16 percent of members of federal and state governments had been in major administrative positions (Steinkemper, 1974: 28). Consequently, the "distance" and potential for conflict between government and administration has been reduced.

The Steinkemper survey reveals a surprisingly high level of heterogeneity and a much closer integration into the social, economic, and political systems than is usually assumed. Heterogeneity becomes more apparent towards the top of the public service where it is most clearly represented by state secretaries at the federal level. Top-level administrative posts are increasingly occupied by people whose backgrounds are nonadministrative and who owe their rapid advancement to a mixture of their expertise and party political motives. Moreover, the post of "political" officials has been used to create a new breed of politicians, *beamtete Politiker*, who achieve a guaranteed income for life without joining the career service even if, like Hans Friederichs, they return to a political career.

Although over half of senior officials interviewed at federal and state levels were party members (Steinkemper, 1974: 48), party politicization has in fact been associated with a greater range of expertise at the top rather than loss of respect for it. Party politicization (along with demographic development) has above all reduced the average age of senior officials to below that of the leadership groups in the economic sphere. No longer does the senior civil service represent the oldest and most conservative of all leadership groups as Wildenmann (1968) suggested. According to Zapf (1966) the average age of state secretaries was 57.4 years. By 1972 the average age of state secretaries had dropped to 50.3 years and was below that of their subordinates, reflecting the fact that they were no longer mainly recruited out of the career service (Steinkemper, 1974: 33). Promotion of able young man by the parties has become a way of overcoming the tendency towards the seniority principle in administration. Party politicization had also brought about an increase of "outsiders" from the late 1960s. This process was not simply associated with SPD ministries but was found more widely, indicating that it reflects a general adaptation to the need for specialists in modern government. The advantages of "outsiders" are clear. They possess a more managerial orientation and a more active role conception; they display a willingness to innovate, a flexible approach to problem solving, and an ability to recognize early developments in highly specialized fields. However, their introduction is likely to produce tensions with traditional administrators, particularly among division heads at the state level who form the oldest, most homogeneous and traditional group.

There is nevertheless a danger of exaggerating how systematic, purposeful, and effective the appointment of "outsiders" was. "Outsiders" were often not present in some of the most important positions for the development and support of major reforms. At the two levels which empirical research (Mayntz and Scharpf, 1973) suggests are the most important in policy development—the subdivision and section (*Referat*) levels—they were much less frequently to be found. In other words, "star" SPD appointees found themselves more often than not reacting to bureaucratic initiatives from below. In a number of important cases "outsiders" failed to make an impact. Examples include Katzer as head of the *Grundsatzabteilung* (central policy division) in the Ministry of Labor and Social Affairs, Claus Noé (former SPD parliamentary party assistant) who was appointed at the age of 31 against much intraministerial opposition as subdivision head for structural policy in the Economics Ministry, and Professor Reimut Jochimsen (from Kiel University, aged 37 on appointment) as chief planner in the Chancellery. Since the early 1970s increased preference has been shown for appointing "outsiders" initially on probation in more junior roles where they can be tested for talent and use to build up a reserve for future promotion. There has been a growing stress on avoiding unnecessary conflict with the bureaucracy and public controversy about personnel affairs.

Just as the traditional jurists' monopoly was related to the Rechtsstaat and the importance of careful application of law in administration, so the growing importance of the "party-book" official is to be understood in terms of the Parteienstaat. The growth of party membership and party identification (not to be equated) at senior levels is also to be understood in terms of the growing party polarization after 1969 with effects on the administration as well as on the general public. In other words it reflected a more general growth of overt party identification. By 1972 over half of the senior officials (state secretaries, heads, and deputy heads of divisions) at the federal and state levels were party members (Steinkemper, 1974: 47). Party membership is not therefore simply confined to "political" officials. Interestingly party membership is higher amongst division heads at the state level ("nonpolitical" officials) than amongst division heads at the federal level ("political" officials). After 1969 the SPD promoted "nonparty" officials to these positions at the federal level because there were too few SPD members in the federal administration to promote. As one goes down the ladder of senior officials in Bonn the proportion of CDU members increases. In 1972 there were no CDU state secretaries. At the level of division head there were two SPD members to every one CDU member; at the level of subdivision head there were two SPD members to every 1.4 CDU members (Steinkemper, 1974: 48). Clearly CDU members were still to be found amongst "political" officials. Party membership and strength of party identification was at its highest amongst "outsiders" who were mainly SPD and mainly to be found at the federal level. A further reason for their introduction was the lack of reservoir of sympathy for the SPD within the federal administration.

In a number of important cases CDU officials were nevertheless left in key administrative positions. For example, in the field of economic policy-making Vogel remained for a period as head of the Grundsatzabteilung in the Finance Ministry despite his vocal opposition to the SPD/FDP government. He was eventually replaced by Manfred Schüler (SPD). Another CDU party-member, Klein, was head of a major tax reform group in the same ministry. At the Economics Ministry, Hans Tietmeyer (CDU) as subdivision head in the EEC division and Kartte as head of the section (Referat) for competition policy remained in their posts. Tietmeyer was later to serve under Hans Friderichs as head of the Grundsatzabteilung whilst Otto Schlecht, a former personal assistant of Erhard's State Secretary Ludger Westrick, was promoted to state secretary. There were many instances of CDU officials ignoring SPD appointees and of SPD appointees ignoring CDU officials for periods of time whilst particular decisions were being prepared. The major reason for leaving CDU officials in their post was political calculation, that is, the need for the support of interest groups close to the CDU/CSU or for Bundesrat support. Threat of a Bundesrat "blockade" could even influence personnel policies.

"Party-book" played a particularly important role in the recruitment of planners to Bonn especially at higher levels (Grottian, 1974). The vast majority came from Berlin, Hamburg, Hesse, and Lower Saxony; notably there were none from Bavaria. Interestingly these new recruits showed that there was still a strong preference fro jurists in key positions presumably on the ground that their skills were necessary to relate planning ideas to bill drafting. The planning of the higher education framework legislation, the urban redevelopment law, and the divorce and penal reforms were undertaken by jurists. Grottian's (1974) survey of Bonn planners found that age and party membership rather than type of educational training correlated most closely with reform interest. Taken as a whole the planners displayed a highly developed political consciousness rather than a technocratic perspective, a reform commitment especially among younger party members, and a left-of-center tendency which led to a relationship of critical and sometimes tense cooperation with political leaders.

Analysis of the states indicates that party patronage has not been introduced by the SPD. Amongst state secretaries SPD members dominate; amongst division heads the CDU dominates. CDU dominance in this latter instance is largely explained by cases like North-Rhine Westphalia where the CDU lost control in 1967 after a long period in government. Thus 87.5 percent of state secretaries in the SPD states and 70.8 percent of state secretaries in the CDU states were members of the governing party. In SPD/FDP states 50 percent of state secretaries were SPD members; 35 percent were FDP members. In the traditional SPD states of Bremen, Hamburg, and Hesse, 70 percent of division heads were SPD members; in the CDU states of Rhineland-Palatinate, Saar, and Schleswig-Holstein, 52.6 percent of division heads were CDU members (Steinkemper, 1974: 49). There were in fact fewer nonparty senior officials especially at the level of division head in SPD states than in CDU states. States like Lower Saxony and North-Rhine Westphalia which had experienced changes of government had a higher than average proportion of nonparty members. Party members had in general better chances of rapid promotion especially SPD members, and in senior posts were on average younger than nonparty members. At the subdivision level of the federal government in 1972 85 percent of SPD members and 87.5 percent of FDP members had been promoted to their present posts since 1969; only 57 percent of CDU officials had been promoted since then (Steinkemper, 1974: 50). Variations can nevertheless be considerable. Whereas the Grand Coalition (CDU/SPD) in Baden-Würtemberg practiced Proporz favoring both SPD and CDU officials, the Grand Coalition in Lower Saxony favored nonparty officials.

In terms of "party sympathy" over 90 percent of the 1972 sample had a clear party preference (Steinkemper, 1974: 55-61).[14] At the federal level nearly one-third of division heads preferred the CDU and more subdivision heads preferred the CDU than the SPD. Below the level of "political" officials in the SPD/FDP states of Lower Saxony and North-Rhine Westphalia there was considerably more support for the CDU than for the SPD. Just half of the officials surveyed showed a strong to very strong party identification, with party identification much stronger at the state than at the federal level. There was evidence of a higher level of party political engagement amongst senior officials than amongst other leadership groups (except the trade unions) despite the fact that other groups did not have the same political restrictions.

Putnam (1973) had concluded from his 1970 survey that senior officials in the Federal Republic were no less egalitarian, liberal, and politically responsive than their British or Swedish counterparts. Using the same statements as Wildenmann in 1968, Steinkemper (1974: 68-80) registered a sharp increase in respect for parliamentarianism and pluralism concluding that senior officials compared favorably with other leadership groups on these dimensions. Party identification correlated with a supportive view of the role of parties in the political process, a more political concept of their role, and especially amongst state secretaries recognition of their own considerable political influence. Respect for politics, norms of tolerance, and political role concepts were much more apparent amongst SPD than CDU members who were on average older and more traditional in outlook. The fewest changes in role conceptions had taken place at the subdivision level, whereas "political" bureaucrats were at their strongest amongst state secretaries particularly in the states. These latter officials had a much more active role conception stressing innovation, commitment to political priorities, and program development.

Most significantly the traditional isolation and autonomy of the higher public service has disappeared. Its degree of integration into the sociopolitical system is reflected in exceptionally high levels of membership (90-100 percent) in organizations and other associations (typically educational and professional), reaching a peak at the level of state secretaries, and in the accumulation of offices (61 percent) in other areas (Steinkemper, 1974: 80-92). Office accumulation is most apparent at the state level particularly in the economic sphere (public enterprises, mixed enterprises, and so forth) and the educational/research sphere. A large proportion of those with industrial offices have already had industrial experience during their careers. Political and party offices are most frequent amongst "political" officials including federal division heads. Party officials are being more frequently appointed to key administrative positions, whilst there is already a tradition of state secretaries transferring to party political careers (for example, Carstens, Ahlers, von Eckardt, Westrick). Over 13 percent of "nonpolitical" officials hold some form of political office; just under 10 percent hold party office. At the same time nearly one-quarter of trade-union leaders and just over 10 percent of leaders of industrial associations hold some form of public service office. The advantage of such integration is that public administration emerges as a major point of contact and source of information for other sectors (Steinkemper, 1974: 92-94). As a clearing house for information it has a real potential for influence on the flow and content of such information. Other leadership groups report more frequent contact with the administrative elite than any other elite. Whilst there may be a mutually beneficial improvement in the flow of information, insight, and flexibility amongst leadership groups, new problems emerge as administrators appear as representatives of particular outside groups within the administration.

Present developments in the public service do of course have their critics. For example, Sontheimer and Bleek (1973) recognize the political role of the public service but regard party political identification as inimical to continuity and trust in the relations between administrators and governments. It is clear that future changes of government at federal and state levels are likely to raise larger problems of loyalty than in 1966 or 1969. In this situation there are no serious proposals for the British model of a larger body of political personnel at the top drawn from parliament. Ministers and parliamentary state secretaries in Bonn number only 35-40, less than half the British figure. Whilst such a solution would enable a "neutral" administration below, it would remove the very real advantages of the German model of the "political" official. In Britain, for example, ministers are much more distracted by the requirements of political office than "political" officials, lack specific qualifications for office, and are therefore less closely integrated into the administrative system. The attempt in the 1960s to shake up traditional "neutralist" attitudes by importation of "irregulars" from the academic and industrial fields was frustrated partly by their incapacity to operate the "machine" and partly by ministers turning to those who could. More interest is shown in Germany in the proposal for extending the definition of "political" officials to cover more senior officials (Steinkemper, 1974: 105). Karl Carstens, a former official and since 1973 leader of the CDU/CSU parliamentary group in the Bundestag, recommended that the opposition might be given in the budget for the Bundestag a number of posts to be filled by "political" officials retired by the government and to provide a nucleus of candidates for such positions on assuming office again. CDU party headquarters in Bonn and CSU headquarters in Munich have already drawn up comprehensive personnel data banks to identify "sympathetic" administrative talent in a more systematic way. By contrast the SPD relies on its *Arbeitsgemeinschaften* (working groups) of jurists and teachers and on the Friedrich Ebert Foundation's list of scholarship students for this purpose.

Whilst the full extent of party politicization of administration is difficult to estimate particularly because of the possibility of rotating officials for "political reasons" it is in fact a cross-party phenomenon. The reason why it is less obvious under CDU than SPD governments is to be understood largely in terms of the histories of these parties. As a product of the historical origins of the SPD as a class party which remained long in opposition there remains a legacy of the view that party membership is an affirmation of one's commitment. Such pressures have not been as strong in the CDU which historically arose as a party of government. It has been able to rely on sympathizers in a range of social groups; church membership, membership in a student corporation, or belonging to some closely related interest group was adequate confirmation of reliability. Also the significance of "party book" was reinforced by the fact that SPD ascendancy in Bonn coincided with the period of retirement of the first postwar administrative generation.

It is easy to exaggerate the extent of unified party control involved in patronage even within the smaller city-states. Promising political figures particularly at the *Land* level emerge as patrons in their own right; ambitious and energetic young officials tend to establish close links with such figures. However, patronage is not only exercised by ministers. Indeed the "patronized," typically senior officials, become patrons in their own right. A chain of patronage is established with a consequently close involvement of officials in party thinking at all levels. It does not follow that this process is centrally directed and controlled. Rather a dynamic and fluid network of relationships involving personal confidences based on shared political conceptions emerges within the administration. Party links within and between ministries forge a new confidential and influential system of communication which the ambitious offical is keen to join.

It is not therefore surprising if party assumes particular importance as a variable influencing administrative behavior. For example, the structure of the party system will influence whether one party dominates patronage (subject to self-restraint and public criticism) or whether there is competition for patronage. Areas of traditional one-party dominance like Bremen, Hamburg, the Saar, and West Berlin assume distinctive characteristics. In Bavaria the claim of the CSU to be the "state party" produces a particularly strong desire for hegemony and a sensitivity to critical views. However, if party dominance in areas like Hamburg, the Saar, or West Berlin has encouraged a "party-book" administration, the increasing electoral volatility apparent in recent years threatens to undermine the phenomenon. Here the FDP has been able to stand as an opponent of patronage and mitigate some of its effects. In states like North-Rhine Westphalia and Lower Saxony which have experienced changes of party control the legacy of previous patronage reinforces contemporary problems of planning and coordination between ministries and produces varying but frequently high levels of suspicion in administrative relationships. Secondly, internal administrative relations are influenced by the climate of inter- and intra-party relations. For example, tensions between Right and Left within the SPD spill over into administrative relationships in Hesse. In other words, systems of one-party dominance are not necessarily associated with easier processes of coordination and control. By contrast the fact that the CDU parties in Rhineland-Palatinate and Schleswig-Holstein are essentially "minister-president parties" with no real doctrinal or personal rivalries has a general effect on the smoothness of administrative relations which even goes beyond "party-book" officials. Another aspect of party influence is the "negative" aspect which in recent years has been restrengthened in the form of the so-called Radicals Decree of 1972. The significance of the Radicals Decree is not to be understood without reference to the "party-book" phenomenon. A strategy of "marching through the institutions" by the radical Left can be partly seen as a response to the fact that the established parties have already established just such as a precedent. This strategy and the reaction of SPD and CDU is to be understood in the German context of the Parteienstaat. Having identified themselves with the state, a threat to the power of existing party leaders is all too easily interpreted as a threat to the state.

"VERFILZUNG" AND THE SOCIAL STRUCTURE
OF PARTIES AND PARLIAMENTS

The major controversy about the use and abuse of party patronage of offices at the state level was to arise in the city-state elections of Hamburg in 1974 and of Bremen and West Berlin in 1975. It was also to be an important theme in the state and local elections in Hesse in 1974 with reference to the Main region cities like Frankfurt and Darmstadt where the CDU complained about the number of left-wingers getting jobs in their SPD city governments. Two factors encouraged the prominence of the theme in the city-states. In the first place, the phenomenon is more concentrated and obvious there because of the high level of party activity compared to other states, the concentration of state and local authority functions (local authorities have traditionally been more affected by patronage) and consequently the large number of posts to be filled, and the close personal contacts possible between ministers and officials particularly through party meetings. An SPD official in Hamburg (1,800,000) or Bremen (700,000) is more likely to come across his minister or administrative superior at party meetings than if he were employed in Hesse (5,300,000) or North-Rhine Westphalia (17,000,000). Second, much of the impetus behind the issue was provided by the Left within the SPD of Berlin, Bremen, and Hamburg who regarded patronage as an instrument of domination by the Right. The issue revealed in fact more about the growing polarization within the SPD than about the polarization between the major parties, for the CDU's exploitation of the issue was hampered by their own involvement in the practice. Curiously the Left provided useful ammunition to the Springer press which was able to use its monopoly of the press in Berlin and Hamburg to seriously embarrass the SPD over this issue.

Filzokratie refers to a complex entanglement of public and private interests at the expense of administrative values of impartiality, equality of treatment, and detachment. The autonomy of administrative action as a basis for the application of objective criteria is waived in favor of political manipulation of governmental powers to secure personal rewards and rewards for party supporters. It is associated with the phenomenon of *Machtverfilzung,* a tangled web of power relationships built up by patronage which frustrates effective internal party debate and parliamentary control over government. Filzokratie is the product of the "party-book" administration. In the case of the city-states, ambitious officials are encouraged to join the SPD to secure promotion prospects. Administrative superiors may frequently expect party political activity from their subordinates for they can use their patronage to silence internal party criticism and to strengthen their individual power base within the party. Internal party opposition can therefore mean career difficulties for an official in the sense that criticism of a party leader can also be interpreted as criticism of one's administrative superior. The consequence is political immobilism and a tendency for the local SPD to degenerate into a "career party of the public service" whose members' major preoccupation is with office and whose major material fear is exclusion from the party. This process has gone furthest in West Berlin where the SPD occupies more posts and offices than anywhere else (Raschke, 1974: 100-107). Administration there is decentralized to districts (*Bezirke*); the party majority on these district councils, whether SPD or CDU, exercises wide party patronage including schools appointments. Typically, SPD left-wing critics are appointed at this level and thereby drawn into the process of entanglement. These "district leftists" find jobs in turn for their colleagues with loyalty being a more important criterion than achievement. The West Berlin situation is not of course surprising considering the long resistance of its SPD to the concept of a career public service; reluctant acceptance of Bonn public service law did little to modify practice. Indeed in the 1950 West Berlin election (which the SPD lost) the "party book" was already a major electoral theme. The phenomenon achieved its tight grip after 1963 when the CDU left the Berlin government and the Grand Coalition was replaced by a SPD/FDP coalition. By contrast in Hamburg in 1974 only four of the nine top administrators, *Staatsräte*, and only one-third at the next level, *Senatsdirektoren*, were members of the SPD. CDU anger in Hamburg was directed at the SPD's abandonment of the traditional Proporz in appointment of the permanent Staatsräte; interestingly in the 1950s Max Brauer had been succeeded for a period as Lord Mayor by his own CDU Staatsrat.

A second feature of Filzokratie is the undermining of parliamentary control over government. One-quarter of the Hamburg state parliament are public employees by background, and in West Berlin the proportion is even higher (two-thirds of the SPD and nearly one-half of the CDU parliamentary parties.) In 1974 over half of the members of West Berlin parliament's construction committee were employees of the Ministry of Construction (*Baubehörde*) and 13 out of 15 members of the interior committee which considers public service issues were officials. Only in three out of 22 committees are ministry representatives in a minority. A further aspect of Filzokratie is the reward to parliamentarians of lucrative posts in state undertakings, such as the Hamburg housing construction authority, building society, water and gas companies (on Hamburg see Barthel, 1973). Such appointments seem, however, to have been examples of "welfare" patronage rather than attempts to extend direct control over these enterprises. Appointment of CDU as well as SPD figures to such state undertakings has if anything served to weaken public criticism and control of their operations. A fourth feature of Filzokratie is that party influence also means influence of associated private economic and industrial interests with consequences for the quality of public planning and the possibility of scandals. Italian-style *parentela* and *clientela* relationships threaten to emerge with a triple selective alliance of party, interests, and bureaucracy. Public service values are in danger of being displaced by private calculations. West Berlin has, for example, been plagued by financial and construction scandals. In Hamburg public criticism of the "privileged" relationship between the trade union construction giant *Neue Heimat* and the Ministry of Construction (Baubehörde) has mounted. Doubt is expressed, for example, about the practice of former Baubehörde officials working for the Neue Heimat. One of the major issues in Bremen's politics during the legislative period 1971-1975 was the Baubehörde's eventually abortive adoption of a Neue Heimat project. Close relations between prominent Hamburg SPD politicians and trade union organizations like *Coop* and *Produktion* have also been the subject of much criticism. A complex web of interdependencies is created in this way which can be used by a narrow political leadership to maximize its control particularly through the one important resource of patronage. In reality *Verfilzung* is more a set of practices which have developed out of the long and close association of party, interests, and bureaucracy than a consciously managed and centrally directed process. In fact it has become a political embarrassment to SPD leaders who recognize that Verfilzung has only further discredited the image of the party. Party patronage is turning from a useful political resource into a potential electoral hazard.

Verfilzung can be viewed as one aspect of the long struggle for control within the Berlin SPD. Patronage was a useful resource for party leaders in this struggle. Despite the overwhelming importance of the working-class vote to SPD success in West Berlin, the participation of workers in the Berlin SPD was by the 1950s significantly below the average for the West German SPD (Raschke, 1974: 101). The proportion of workers in the Berlin SPD has continued to decline more rapidly than at the federal level, whilst the proportion of public officials has increased substantially faster than at the federal level. By contrast to changes in the population structure and in the SPD vote the consequence is a growing underrepresentation of workers and overrepresentation of public employees. In such "workers districts" as Kreuzberg there has been a growing tendency for public functionaries to dominate local party activity. In Kreuzberg 54 percent of the SPD district council members and 78 percent of the district's delegates to the state party conference in 1971 were public employees (Raschke, 1974: 338). Whereas in the Charlottenburg district 2.2 percent of SPD members were public employees in 1952, this figure had increase to 29 percent by 1968 (Raschke, 1974: 341). Moreover as one climbs the party hierarchy the number of public employees in key positions increases. They accounted for 47.7 percent in 1951 and 53.1 percent in 1974 of delegates to the SPD state party conference. Indeed according to the SPD only four of the 254 delegates in 1974 were workers. It is not, therefore, surprising if local party leaders are sought out by party members for assistance with a wide variety of problems—housing, pensions, jobs and careers, legal problems, and welfare generally. Such leaders can help either because they possess expertise in specific policy fields or because they have personal contacts amongst party colleagues in the relevant administrative positions as well as intimate knowledge of how the machinery operates.

Verfilzung has had two consequences for the SPD party leadership, one "positive" and one "negative." First, assimilation of dissent into the state apparatus is an important technique for reducing internal party conflict. Most of the districts are controlled by the Right, but in districts such as Kreuzberg, Schöneberg, and Tiergarten there have been long periods of control by the Left. Whilst there is an overwhelming tendency for right-wingers to be appointed and promoted at the state level—where because the major decisions are reached here political loyalty is regarded as essen-tial—the Left do quite well at the district level. Their presence at the dis-trict level can be interpreted as an attempt by the Right to "muzzle" criticism. A far more serious consequence for the party leadership was revealed in the 1975 West Berlin election. Unlike any other state election of 1974-1975 the largest SPD losses were amongst workers (Schmollinger, 1975). It could be claimed that as a product of Verfilzung the SPD in West Berlin was doing even less than the SPD at the federal level to represent worker interests. The SPD search to appeal to the "new middle class" diminished the distance between it and the CDU and eased the transfer of working class votes to the CDU in 1975. Largest CDU gains were made in the "worker" districts of the city, whereas SPD losses were lowest in districts where there was an above average proportion of Beamte and Angestellte. In Kreuzberg where there has been much urban renewal SPD losses were greatest and the small parties did very well. Here the right-wing *Bund Freies Deutschland* got 4.2 percent of the vote, whilst in some constituencies of this district the communist SEW (Socialist Unity Party of West Berlin) got over 18 percent of the vote. There was a loss to the SPD of over 20 percent in Kreuzberg since 1971 compared to just over 11 percent in middle-class Zehlendorf.

As a phenomenon Verfilzung is not exclusive to the SPD and the city-states. It is useful to compare Hamburg with its neighbor Schleswig-Holstein, a classic case of CDU Verfilzung. Here successive CDU and CDU-dominated governments have pursued an aggressive personnel policy, more party conscious and centrally directed than in other states. In the early

1950s, for example, Minister-President Friedrich Lübke responded to intense pressures from the CDU party organization by intervening frequently in personnel policy especially in the Schools Ministry and the division of the Interior Ministry dealing with personnel policy for the state. Close relations were established between the party and the Interior Ministry to offset the effects of SPD patronage between 1947 and 1950. Between 1950 and 1953 not one single SPD party member was appointed to the state administration. The new Minister-President Uwe von Hassel in 1954 established in his State Chancellery a coordinating office for personnel policy under an official drawn in from the party organization, and in 1956 the party was involved even more fully in personnel policy through "contact men" in each ministry. Interior Minister Lemke (Minister-President from 1963) ensured that party demands for patronage were fully satisfied. An important contributory factory was the influence of BHE strength and competition for the large refugee vote on CDU personnel policy; absorption of the former by the latter meant adoption of its patronage policies. By contrast in Rhineland-Palatinate (CDU) the BHE was never a serious competitor to the CDU and consequently the latter has never pursued so vigorous a personnel policy.

After 1970 under Minister-President Gerhard Stoltenberg, who as chairman of Schleswig-Holstein's *Junge Union* (Young Union) in the 1950s had advocated an active CDU personnel policy, this policy was to be reinforced. For the first time the CDU ruled alone. "Party book" became an election issue in 1975 when the chairman of the Landtag party, Uwe Barschel, was quoted as saying with respect to educational appointments: "It must become obvious but without too much publicity that our government regards its CDU friends as the most suited to apply CDU policies locally" (CDU im Landtag, 1974). Schleswig-Holstein operates a very centralized schools policy which actively promotes CDU teachers notably as headmasters. Such patronage is not new; for a long time CDU Ministers of Education in North-Rhine Westphalia were criticized for favoring Catholics. It also accords with the increased politicization of educational appointments as radical politically active teachers have emerged and as views on structure, methods and content of education have polarized. There have, for example, been growing complaints about the active intervention of Baden-Würtemberg's Education Ministry since 1972 in the autonomy of university staffing decisions in order to favor CDU members or sympathizers.

There are three important differences in personnel policy between Hamburg and Schleswig-Holstein. First, the State Chancellery in Kiel has a much stronger sense of political engagement than the Senate Chancellery in Hamburg.[15] Close relations are cultivated with the CDU through the section (Referat) on personnel planning and the section dealing with party and interest group relations. In other states the latter function is given to a personal assistant of the minister-president or of his state secretary rather than embedded in the normal administrative structure. Whereas the State Chancellery in "Red" Hesse has a CDU division head (coordination division), the Schleswig-Holstein Chancellery does not have a single SPD official in any position of authority. A second difference is that personnel policy in Hamburg is opened up to public view through the *Deputationen* (deputations), bodies of co-opted individuals who advise the ministries (*Behörde*). These advisory bodies help to avoid the worst abuses of party political practice by providing a forum in which open disagreement can take place between party representatives over appointments. By contrast Schleswig-Holstein possesses a very centralized personnel policy directed from the center which has been used to introduce party criteria systematically into appointments and promotions. A further example of openness and democratization of personnel policy in Hamburg is provided by the progressive school constitution law of 1973 which reduces the role of the Schools Ministry by providing for participation of teachers, pupils, and parents in the appointment (for only five years at a time) of headmasters. By contrast in Schleswig-Holstein appointments with security of tenure are made centrally after hearing local views. In the latter system it is much more easy to introduce and implement party political criteria. The strength of party patronage in Schleswig-Holstein compared, for example, to Rhineland-Palatinate or even Hamburg is very much a reflection of the local political culture. This culture is influenced primarily by the postwar refugee population and by the strength within the CDU of the interests of powerful farmers through the *Bauernverband* (Varain, 1964). "Welfare" patronage has been reinforced by a high level of polarization between CDU and SPD compared to Rhineland-Palatinate.

The issue of Verfilzung raises the problem of the social structure of the political parties which seems to reflect the existence of the Parteienstaat. In October 1968 Beamte accounted for 9.9 percent of SPD members at the federal level compared to 5 percent in 1952. Workers (*Arbeiter*) accounted for 34.5 percent in the same year (dropping in 1973 to 26.43 percent) compared to 45 percent in 1952 (Schmollinger, 1974: 62). In other words, the proportion of workers within the SPD had fallen much more rapidly than their share of the total working population (7 percent between 1952 and 1970). Only 27.6 percent of new entrants in 1972 were workers compared to 51.4 percent in 1965 (Schmollinger, 1974: 65). The SPD has become more attractive for Beamte and Angestellte (employees) in the public service, but particularly since joining the Grand Coalition in

1966 has had a rapid fall in the proportion of workers in its membership. Nevertheless, 66 percent of workers voted SPD in 1972 compared to 54 percent in 1965 and only 48 percent in 1953. Schmollinger has, however, described the 1972 election an "an election without alternatives" for the workers. A study commissioned by the Hamburg SPD found that one of six factors governing entry into the party was "the SPD as governing party." There the proportion of new members who are workers fell from 30.9 percent in 1964-1965 to 18.8 percent in 1971. Between 1964 and 1971 workers averaged 23 percent and Beamte 14.3 percent of new members. In 1970 15.2 percent of new members were Beamte. The increase of students from 6.8 percent of new members to 23.7 percent of new members in 1971 reflected new problems and further reinforced the gap between the structure of party membership and the social structure of Hamburg. In the case of West Berlin Beamte and Angestellte in the public service accounted for 19.2 percent of new SPD members in 1971 compared to 10.8 percent at the federal level (Schmollinger, 1975: 448).

Just as the SPD's social structure shows a tendency towards public servants when in government (for example, in West Berlin and Hamburg), a similar tendency is apparent in the CDU. As the traditional party of government at the federal level, public servants are well represented. In 1955 Beamte accounted for 9 percent of total membership; by October 1968 this figure had risen to 15.8 percent. Whereas in 1955 there had been a larger proportion of workers than Beamte (15 percent to 9 percent), the situation had been reversed in 1968 with only 13.1 percent workers (Schmollinger, 1974: 66). In the traditional SPD state of Hamburg only 7.4 percent of CDU members were Beamte in 1975 compared to 16.7 percent in the traditional CDU state of Rhineland-Palatinate. Interestingly the proportion of Beamte in the FDP dropped from 15 percent in 1965 when it was in the federal government to 8 percent in 1967 when it was in opposition and rose again by 1971 to the extraordinarily high proportion of 19.6 percent (Schmollinge, 1974: 71). Clearly it would be crude to suggest that these figures merely reflect job opportunism. They also reflect the appeal made by party policies to different occupational groups. The SPD remains a party of workers and lower-level public servants, the CDU is a party of the self-employed, farmers, and mainly middle-level public servants, whilst the FDP represents the "aristocracy of workers" including higher-level public servants. In membership terms the CSU is a party of the "petit bourgeoisie" with Beamte accounting for only 7 percent of its membership in 1964 (workers accounted for only 2 percent). Nevertheless Beamte are strongly overrepresented in all parties: 8.8 percent of Beamte belong to a political party, a far higher proportion than for any other occupational group. Only 2.4 percent of workers are organized in parties (Schmollinger, 1974: 76). Clearly much of this difference is to be explained in terms of educational levels. Even so these figures represent a remarkable degree of identify of interests between parties and public servants. Electoral success of a party is bound up with career expectations of its members. Hence in 1968 public servants accounted for 19.5 percent of SPD and 18.6 percent of CDU membership. As a proportion of wage-earners in the party public servants accounted for 32.3 percent of those in the SPD and 54.2 percent of those in the CDU although only some 15 percent of wage-earners fall within the category "direct public service" and another 8 percent in the category "indirect public service" (Schmollinger, 1974: 78).

Public service employment is also an excellent base from which to achieve party office or election to public office. In the SPD in 1968 Beamte accounted for 9.9 percent of party members, 19.7 percent of party members elected to public office, and 18.5 percent of those in party offices. Workers (34.3 percent of members) did well in terms of party office (34.8 percent) but less well in terms of elected office (25.8 percent). Within the CDU Beamte accounted for 15.8 percent of members, 30.3 percent of those elected to public office (workers 3 percent, self-employed 51.5 percent) and 33.3 percent of those in party offices (workers 6.7 percent, self-employed 30 percent). Clearly Beamte are even more strongly represented in party and public offices than amongst the general membership; this is especially true of the CDU (Schmollinger, 1974: 79). Parties of government prefer to promote those with public service expertise directly relevant to their tasks. Consequently the interests of workers tend to be filtered out within the parties which become less attractive to workers. Moreover in controversial questions public servants can be better relied on than industrial workers or lower-level white collar workers to support the party leadership. Workers are a marginal group in the CDU (11 percent in 1973 compared to 28 percent self-employed) and FDP (4.9 percent in 1971) and of declining significance in the SPD. The latter feature is not surprising as the SPD has sought to become a *Volkspartei* encompassing a wide range of interests rather than simply workers' interests.

Wage-earners, whether organized in trade unions or not, see their interests best represented by trade unions, followed by works councils (*Betriebsräte*) with the SPD a very poor third (on the Infas survey of 1970, see Schmollinger, 1974: 82). The DGB (German Trade Union Federation) has in recent years succeeded much more than the SPD in attracting workers. Whilst the proportion of workers organized in trade unions fell between 1950 and 1968 (from 40.4 percent to 39.7 percent), it had reached a record figure of 42 percent for the DGB in 1972. Meanwhile between 1968 and 1973 the proportion of trade unionists within the parties has fallen as the proportion of public servants and young people has risen (students accounted for nearly 16 percent of SPD members in 1972). The entry of the SPD into the Grand Coalition in 1966 and the economic crisis of the mid-1960s seemed to be the turning-point in relations between the workers and the political parties. Whereas the SPD firmly rejected the unofficial strikes of the late 1960s, the trade unions as direct representatives of worker interests reacted much more sympathetically. By the mid-1970s it had become clear that the traditional identity of interest between DGB and SPD could no longer be taken for granted. Critics of the Parteienstaat and of the SPD as a *Staatspartei* sought reform strategies outside the traditional party framework, seeing the possibility of turning the trade unions from an *Ordnungsfaktor* (force for order) preserving social and economic peace to a *Gegenmacht* or adversary power (Schmidt, 1971).

Verfilzung is reflected in the social structure of parliaments as well as of parties. Criticisms of the bureaucratization of West German parliaments have been partly directed at the ever increasing division of labor affecting their work and that of the parliamentary parties. It has also been directed at the *Verbeamtung der Parlamente,* their reduction to assemblies of officials. There is, as mentioned above, a German parliamentary tradition of the *Beamtenabgeordnete:* the public servant as parliamentarian. A variety of factors play a part in this phenomenon: their privileges, knowledge, and financial security make them attractive to parties; there remains still a high level of popular trust in the Beamte; and of course complex career and political motives enter into the choice of so many officials to seek a parliamentary seat. It may be that a public service career is associated with a concern for public affairs and communal problems which is a stronger motive than financial inducements for seeking a political career. Since 1949 there has been a steady increase of Beamte in the Bundestag. Whereas in 1957 they amounted to 24 percent (29 percent including Angestellte in the public service) of parliamentarians, this figure had risen by 1972 to 31 percent (39 percent including Angestellte). Of the 31 percent Beamte, just under one-third were teachers and academics. They form the largest single occupational group in the Bundestag; Angestellte in the private sector come second with 25.7 percent (Hess, 1976: 36). In fact their percentage increase in the Bundestag reflects no more than their percentage increase within the population. Few changes have taken place since the late 1950s in the distribution between different types of Beamte. Local elected Beamte (such as mayors, *Landräte*), "political" officials, and older higher-ranking Beamte have given way somewhat to younger members of the higher service (*höherer Dienst*), to members of the superior service (*gehobener Dienst*) and to teachers (Hess, 1976: 36). In other words, a traditionally homogeneous elitist group of Beamtenabgeordnete has been replaced by a more representative group in age and hierarchical terms. As they are evenly distributed between the parties (with the exception of their underrepresentation in the FDP parliamentary party) they do not form a unified group in the Bundestag. One striking feature of recent years has been the emergence amongst younger members of the higher service in the Bundestag of a new type of career politician.

The view that overrepresentation of Beamte has reached a critical level is reinforced by the state parliaments (*Landtage*). In the Bundestag the danger of role conflict for Beamte is less great; it is not only a very heterogeneous group but also contains many Beamte drawn from *Land,* or local authority service. By contrast a far larger proportion of Beamte in state parliaments are employed by the state concerned. In 1975 Beamte and Angestellte in the public service accounted for an average 46 percent of state parliament seats. Such high figures are not new. In 1959, for example, Bremen and Hesse had proportions of over 50 percent. However, in the 1970s this trend has increased markedly. Despite the introduction of new regulations on incompatibility of offices (that is, for local elected Beamte in the Landtage) in states like Hesse and the Saar, there has not been a proportionate fall in their representation. These officials have been replaced mainly by teachers. Improved parliamentary allowances particularly in Bavaria from 1970 have also had no observable effect. The largest increase has been amongst teachers who account on average for just one-third of the Beamte/Angestellte group. Parties appreciate the flexible leisure-time available to the teacher for political activity (encouraged by German school hours), whilst teachers have been drawn into political activity by the increasing politicization of education. It is interesting to note the range of distribution of the proportion of public officials between states in 1975. Five states exceeded the 50 percent threshold: Hesse (61 percent), the Saar (58 percent), Baden-Würtemberg (54 percent), Bavaria (53 percent) and Rhineland-Palatinate (52 percent). As only Hesse is SPD (it has in fact a SPD/FDP government), the phenomenon is certainly not just associated with the SPD. In 1975 only one CDU state, Schleswig-Holstein (43 percent), fell below the 50 percent barrier. North-Rhine Westphalia had 41.5 percent, Lower Saxony 38 percent, Berlin 40 percent, Hamburg 37.5 percent, and Bremen 33 percent. These variations are to be partly explained in terms of local political climate. Thus, Hesse (particularly Hesse South) has a much more intellectual tradition of politics than Hamburg or Bremen, where trade-unionists play a more important role in the parliamentary parties. These two city-states reflect in the social structure of their parliaments a tradition of *Kaufmannssozialismus* (commercial socialism) which is not apparent in Hesse. By contrast, Bavaria has a much more patriarchal and paternalist style of politics which is reflected in the high esteem of the public service. Almost all Bavarian ministers since 1946 have held posts before in the Bavarian administration.

It is not surprising if the role of public servants in politics has become more controversial in recent years. The principle of separation of powers is clearly endangered when so many legislators are recruited from the executive. In addition legislation is likely to suffer from too much influence by administrative considerations. For example, it can be argued that in the Bundestag too much time and energy is expended on detail and too little on the political contents and implications of issues. Parliament, even to a considerable extent the opposition, becomes "a partner of the federal government in the area of executive power" through its committees (Thaysen, 1975: 33). Detailed work in a spirit of partnership accounts for the high proportion of bills which are passed unanimously. Consequently the question is sometimes raised whether the legislative diligence of the Bundestag is so necessary or whether there is a tendency to regulate matters which do not always require statutory regulation. Beamtenabgeordneten are noted for their particular diligence in filling out long government draft bills with even greater detail. Far more controversial is the public complaint summed up in the term "self-service shop" by former Federal President Gustav Heinemann (Der Spiegel, 1974: 14). Beamtenabgeordneten are frequently pictured as a lobby within parliament which unashamedly creates advantages for itself. Retention of the political privileges of officials, generous noncontributory pensions, rapidly rising personnel costs in the public sector, and a whole host of financial advantages secured through the interior committees are cited as evidence of this form of "self-service." Of the 27 members of the interior committee during the seventh Bundestag 15 were Beamte. One abuse of the public service law perpetrated by 21 Beamtenabgeordneten in 1972 was to resign one's seat just before the end of the legislative period and re-enter the public service to receive immediate promotion. After paid election leave and re-election, the official re-entered parliament with a higher allowance. In North-Rhine Westphalia Beamte were estimated in 1953 to receive 115 financial concessions (Der Spiegel, 1974: 36). Beyond such official concessions there was an informal but dramatic process of rapid promotion within career groups without changes of duty. There has been in recent years an enormous transition of officials from salary group A16 to B3 (B is the highest salary group). In 1966 at the federal level all *Ministerialräte* (*Referenten* in the ministries) were paid at A16; in 1971 three-quarters were being paid at B3. Such rapid promotion of younger officials creates frustration below as the top of *Laufbahngruppen* (career groups) get more and more overcrowded year by year. Problems also arise about how to employ so many highly paid officials in equivalent jobs. Career frustrations are further exacerbated by increased recruitment of "outsiders" by ministers and consequent problems of reorganization of work to provide a useful job for those recruited once the minister departs. The consequence is often complex and fanciful organizational constructions (as in the Economics Ministry after Schiller's departure) which bear no relation to criteria of rational administration. One further practice which causes public resentment is the widespread promotion of "unwanted" officials in order to encourage them to retire earlier with a higher pension. Tolerance for such advantages and sometimes "abuses" is clearly excessive. It is, therefore, hardly surprising if the Federal Republic has witnessed an enormous increase in official posts. Between 1960 and 1970 the number of senior officials in North-Rhine Westphalia increased from 117 to 414, in Bavaria from 95 to 338.

The social structure of the parties and parliaments helps to explain the difficulties of public service reform in the wake of the report in 1973 of the Study Commission for the Reform of Public Service Law. Unlike reform of the British civil service, the scope of such a reform, the politicized nature of its object, and the fact that the public service would to a greater extent be reforming itself made it a very divisive political issue. Successive FDP Interior Ministers, Hans Genscher and Werner Maihofer, who were responsible for public service reform, could not afford to forget that 19 percent of their party membership comprised Beamte and that the Beamte vote (one and a half million) was very important for the FDP. In fact the 1973 report favored Genscher's view; his State Secretary, Günter Hartkopf, as chairman of the Study Commission used his casting vote to ensure that Arbeiter (workers) and Angestellte (employees) were included in the category of Beamte. In other words the *Berufsbeamtenum* and its privileges was to be maintained and indeed extended. Its abolition would require constitutional amendment anway. Arbeiter and Angestellte were to be offered greater job security but at the expense of loss of collective bargaining rights and the right to strike. The Beamte in the Interior Ministry responsible for preparing reforms were themselves not disposed towards radical reform. Under Genscher a seven-year "realization plan" and under Maihofer an "action program" were formulated to relate pay to job evaluation and achievement rather than to seniority and to abolish the traditional distinction between simple, middle, superior, and higher services in favor of groupings based on function. The traditional distinction had been based on formal educational qualifications rather than the job done. These proposals sought to ensure that the same work would be paid equally and not differently because one belonged to a different grade; they even sought to make senior positions temporary and provide for the possibility of dismissal. The fact that even such a "small" reform proved abortive before 1976 was also due to the SPD which did not want to awaken conflict within its own ranks between trade union and Beamte views by giving prominence to the issue. It would be difficult to resolve the basic disagreement between DGB and DBB over public service reform as the Study Commission itself illustrated. Nine of its 19 members favored the DGB's hostility to the privileges of the Beamte in favor of a single service law abolishing the traditional distinction between Arbeiter, Angestellte, and Beamte and giving to all public servants the right to strike and rights of collective bargaining (both denied to Beamte). Reform would, of course, raise difficult technical problems, for example the lack of an agreed evaluation system to measure and compare results within the public service. More significant are the political problems raised by the financial threat to train drivers, postmen, refuse collectors, and many parliamentarians. Unlike civil service reform in Britain, the scope of the German public service and the extent to which it "enmeshes" German politics and society make its reform a potentially very divisive political issue.

THE "PARTY-BOOK" BROADCASTING CORPORATIONS

A far more serious threat to institutional autonomy and professional values is posed by the interference of the political parties in radio and television broadcasting particularly since 1969. Broadcasting is the responsibility of 11 public-law bodies whose management is independent of government in order to emphasize their public service role and their moral educative function. As broadcasting is held by the Constitutional Court to fall within the states' exclusive jurisdiction over cultural affairs,[16] the broadcasting companies were established either by state law or as in the case of the *Norddeutscher Rundfunk* by interstate treaty. The Second German Television Service (ZDF) is also founded and regulated by interstate treaty as a separate station. Finance is mainly from license fees, and in a judgment of 1971 the Federal Administrative Court doubted that a private commercial broadcasting system would be constitutional.

The obvious gap between legislative intent and the reality of party political influence within the broadcasting companies has caused increasing anxiety in recent years. Although state parliaments elect the members of the broadcasting councils, statute limits the number of parliamentarians who can be elected and expressly requires members to be drawn from various social groups. In fact the parliamentary parties have sought to place reliable party members on these councils. The broadcasting councils in turn elect the supervisory boards who choose with the council's approval the director-general (*Intendant*) and approve key appointments. Through this process of election and approval of appointments, party influence has been able to extend deep into the corporations with potentially serious consequences. Three types of broadcasting corporation have developed:

(1) There is the *Westdeutscher Rundfunk* (WDR) whose non-party director-general, Klaus von Bismarck, has resolutely defended his corporation from party political influence in favor of professional journalistic values.

(2) There are the corporations of one-party dominance such as the "Red" stations like Bremen or Hesse or the "Black" stations like Saar, South-West, and South-German.

(3) There are the stations characterized by *Proporz* politics. In the case of ZDF (Second German Television) the advantage lies with the CDU, whereas in the NDR there is more of a party balance; in both cases a director-general or one party (SPD in the NDR, CDU in the ZDF) is complemented by a deputy from the other major party; the problem at NDR is party deadlock (there is a "pat" situation on the broadcasting council) and blockade tactics are used, particularly by the CDU with respect to appointments.

As the corporations combine to produce the first program through a joint institution, the ARD, many of the party anxieties with respect to the "bias" in the media are the product of this institution. As a consequence of the combined first program conservative states like Bavaria and Baden-Würtemberg have been unable to protect themselves from outside critical analysis. These two states have frequently complained of the dominance of the "Red North" in ARD and sought a greater role for the two CDU stations, South-German and South-West, and for the Bavarian Broadcasting Corporation within ARD. Hence ARD has been subjected to greater political pressures than ever before. The key problems have been associated with NDR and WDR which play major roles in the first program. Current affairs programs like *Panorama* (from NDR) and *Monitor* (from WDR) have become notorious to the CDU/CSU. *Panorama's* analysis of affinities between the CDU/CSU and the neo-Nazi NPD and of Strauss's political style produced a political "cause célèbre" in 1969. After three organizers of *Panorama* had either resigned or been dismissed, Peter Merseburger, the new head, was hounded by CDU members of NDR's broadcasting council.

Even NDR's *Tagesschau,* a news magazine produced by a CDU broadcaster, did not please the CSU, the CDU's Bavarian sister-party. The "Filbinger Paper" of 1975, produced by the Baden-Würtemberg government, criticized *Tagesschau's* orientation to federal affairs and stressed the need to regionalize its production. According to this paper, far greater prior information needed to be given about program contents so that individual stations could withdraw from ARD for particular programs. In 1974 the NDR suffered from a leadership crisis when the SPD Director-General Schroder was not reelected because of CDU opposition before his contract expired. The SPD pressed successfully for a party figure, declining for example the CDU's proposal of the "non-party" ambassador in London (who had been a state secretary in Bonn during the CDU years of power). Despite CDU hostility to Merseburger, the director-general (CDU) of the ZDF continued to defend the equally controversial right-wing commentator Gerhard Löwenthal of *ZDF-Magazin* (a current affairs program) from appeals for his dismissal both from inside as well as outside ZDF. It is just not possible to find controversial political commentators like Löwenthal or Merseburger on British television. Such figures help reinforce party fears that broadcasters are turning into a "third force" in politics with influence not just on the balance of presentation, but also on the agenda of politics. Their selection and ordering of issues puts politicians on the defensive and can therefore aggravate them.

Increased political controversy about political broadcasting was reflected in the "Hammerschmidt Paper" of 1970 on the content of political programs and in the so-called "statutes movement" of program staff to protect their freedom of reporting (Williams, 1976). Hammerschmidt as a CDU director-general of the South-West station and then chairman of ARD produced a somewhat restrictive paper based on his anxieties about the poor standards of political reporting in the first program. This paper was the subject of much controversy which led eventually to an ARD report of a far more liberal nature. Nevertheless tensions continued within ARD with, for example, the South-West station complaining in 1975 about WDR coverage of a demonstration against the Baden-Würtemberg government. The "statutes movement" was a movement of program staff against internal editorial censorship from above. It began within WDR in 1969 after public criticism of WDR coverage of a student demonstration before the Education Ministry in Düsseldorf. Criticism was directed at the failure of WDR staff to make available to the public authorities their knowledge of the demonstration. One suggestion was that television staff be given the status and duties of civil servants. The reaction among WDR staff spread to all other stations where draft statutes were drawn up. It was not, however, a cohesive movement. In fact only NDR adopted such a statute. Elsewhere guidelines were published by the authorities in an effort to incorporate these demands. A further indication of increased controversy was the greater engagement of the churches in broadcasting. The *Proporz* model of the broadcasting councils was still sufficiently a reality for the influence of the churches in broadcasting to be maintained if not increased in recent years. In questions of sex, marriage, divorce, abortion, and education, the Catholic Church in particular has had much to find disquieting in broadcasting and has sought to redouble its influence.

By far the most spectacular broadcasting affair was the so-called "seizure of power" by the CSU in the Bavarian Broadcasting Corporation in 1971-1972. The nomination by the CSU of a state secretary in the Bavarian government as future director-general was followed by a bill from the CSU parliamentary party in the state parliament which drastically increased the number of parliamentarians and gave extra seats to certain pressure groups (not the trade unions) on the broadcasting council. The enlarged broadcasting council was also to be given greater authority to approve leading appointments in the corporation. According to the CSU, parliamentarians were best able to represent audience interests. CSU criticism was chiefly directed at "left-wing and occasionally radical-left collectives" within broadcasting and in particular at the fact that only 23 out of 2,000 employees of the corporation were members of the CSU (Ellwein, 1973: 134). It was felt to be essential to secure CSU influence before the impending federal election in 1973. The bill aroused enormous protest from the SPD, journalist associations, the broadcasting council and director-general, Evangelical and Catholic Churches, and the Senate. As a consequence the CSU failed to pass the bill before the period of the existing council terminated. The CSU then began to consider plans for an alternative private broadcasting system. However, the threat of an impending referendum on a proposal for a constitutional amendment to forbid private broadcasting and reduce the number of state representatives in broadcasting caused the CSU eventually to concede to the political risks of their venture. Appointment of the new director-general was nevertheless followed by personnel changes and program adjustments to suit CSU policy. Bavaria has since threatened (although not convincingly) to pull out of the joint first program.

Perhaps most symbolic of the threats facing German broadcasting was the use of the theme *Rotfunk* ("Red Station") by the CDU/CSU in the North-Rhine Westphalia state election of spring 1975. The CDU/CSU had become increasingly sensitive to the contents of radio and television since its loss of power in 1969. Under Kurt Biedenkopf's direction two experts were employed at CDU headquarters to monitor broadcasts and write reprimands to offending broadcasters. The opposition argued that the SPD had made the fullest use of the opportunities presented by the media to influence public opinion during its long period of opposition. Bias towards the Left in broadcasting led to favorable reporting on government activities and further penalties for a conservative opposition. The CDU/CSU began to search in earnest for influence in the field of broadcasting by exerting pressure through its party members on the broadcasting councils and by exploring the possibilities of a private commercial system. A commercial system was appealing because of the identity of interest with the newspaper and industrial interests supporting such a proposal and the consequent political reliability of programs. However, the CDU/CSU preference for their own direct influence was revealed by the WDR (*Rotfunk*) affair in spring 1975. A prominent CDU member (von Windelen) of the WDR's broadcasting council attacked the corporation's dominance by left-wing intellectuals and claimed that the state election offered an opportunity for a thorough purge of broadcasting personnel (through a newly elected broadcasting council) and for more rigorous central guidance of programs. After the election (which failed to return a CDU majority) the WDR came under increased criticism from director-generals of other corporations through ARD for some of its controversial programs. In fact under von Bismarck and television director Hofer, both non-party, WDR producers and directors had operated with considerable freedom to experiment. Vitality and innovation were certainly given preference over attempts to establish centrally overall impartiality of reporting.

Despite party politicization of broadcasting the media remain remarkably healthy, offering probably the best television in Continental Europe. Compared to France the danger of undue influence for one political grouping is restricted by the federal system. Competition between stations produces beneficial results in terms of standards and experimentation. ARD's first program is on the whole varied and fairly balanced and has improved since ZDF competition started in 1963. Director-generals have tended to be independent-minded and to defend their staff. For example, the CDU chairman of ARD, Hans Bausch, has stubbornly protected the independence of programs like *Tagesschau* and was publicly critical of the "Filbinger Paper." Their terms of office tend to be relatively lengthy, and they cannot be dismissed at the pleasure of the government (only for serious reasons and by special majority of the broadcasting council). One is struck above all by the vigor of current affairs programs compared to their British equivalents; their style is influenced by the different party political environment of German broadcasting. There is less of the British tendency to establish an agreed settlement on issues, much more confrontation of views. Broadcasters are not so much synthesizers on British lines, but tend to associate themselves more with particular points of view. Even so the search for party dominance or the practice of Proporz politics gives ground for concern to political journalists. In the first place, party influence undermines hierarchical controls within the corporations. Increasing influence of parties at lower levels means that employees depend less on the favor of the hierarchy and more on party headquarters. The traditional difficulties of managing broadcasting corporations are accordingly exacerbated. Second, the rule of anticipated reactions comes into play. The possibility of party interventions creates within the corporations an insecurity which can only cramp exploration and the clarification of issues. Political journalism could be strangled within the straightjacket of party identification of their own interests with the general interest. Party control is likely to narrow the horizons of public debate. Certainly the CSU's search for party dominance in Bavaria illustrated very clearly the threat to the quality of public discussion.

THE DANGERS OF THE PARTY STATE

Lack of sympathy to parliamentarianism is not the only attribute of the Parteienstaat. The right to existence of an autonomous neutral professional sphere in public life is also not easy to reconcile with the German concept of the Parteienstaat. Such a professional sphere is autonomous of party constraints and serves to broaden or deepen perspectives. It is traditionally represented by the impartial detached advice of civil servants, the media's criteria of fairness, impartiality, and objectivity, and of course by the courts. There are two fears concerning the Parteienstaat:

(1) It will lower the quality of public debates by narrowing horizons. Interests will only become politically significant in so far as they operate through the parties; as a consequence there may be a problem of tolerance of dissent particularly if expressed outside the established party framework (Dyson, 1975b).

(2) Institutions will be permeated and no longer used for the purposes for which they were originally established.

For example, in the Parteienstaat the loyalty of civil servants to an incoming government can no longer be taken for granted. The Bundesrat may defend the CDU/CSU party program rather than the federal system; its contribution of administrative expertise could be displaced by party polemics. Parties are in danger of establishing a hegemony, becoming "crypto-state" organs which seek to extend their influence over all organs of opinion formation notably broadcasting. Conservative thinkers tend therefore to equate "democratization" with little more than further party politicization at the expense of institutional independence and professional values (Schelsky, 1974). They fear that the balance between political, administrative, and judicial values is endangered. Where administrative and judicial values are respected, anxieties about the consequences of party politicization are natural. How for example can administrative ethics of equity, impartiality, and equality of treatment be safeguarded in a "party-book" bureaucracy?

The degree of permeation of other institutions by the parties is to be largely explained in terms of the historical problems of the German party tradition—in particular the problem of relating "party" and "state." A solution to this problem has been found in the Federal Republic by integration of party and bureaucracy, by mutual accommodation through interlocking rather than by recognition of separate spheres. This solution was implicit in the dual character of the Parliamentary Council as a body dominated both by party representatives and by senior officials. Three-fifths of its members were Beamte. The traditional weakness of German parties in the constitutional tradition made it difficult for the parties to accept the concept of an autonomous neutral administrative system. Bureaucratic claims to neutrality were associated in the past with the *Obrigkeitsstaat*, the sovereign state which claimed to stand "above party." The alternative to the Parteienstaat was seen to be the Obrigkeitsstaat; a neutral bureaucracy threatened to become "a state within a state." Neutrality cannot then mean an administration "beyond" or "above" party, only one subordinated to party. There is no equivalent to the British concept of the Crown as the nonpartisan focus of civil service loyalty. Loyalty to the constitution means recognition of the superior claims of the parties legitimized in Article 21. West Germany represents a different response to the problem of neutrality in the public service. In Britain there has been a search for a nonpartisan public service, whereas in Germany fears of a partisan public service (that is, one dominated by the CDU at the federal level or by the SPD in broadcasting) has tended to produce either the search for control by one's own party or demands for a bipartisan service. Majority and Proporz principles compete at the expense of institutional autonomy.

These historical factors were reinforced by the circumstances of origin of the new republic and by features of the new political system. In the years after 1945 the parties had not only established a moral ascendancy but also were able to offer material services to a distressed population. The welfare function of the parties was to become one method of attracting support and continues to be a major feature of party patronage. There was then the demonstration effect of patronage: the "patronized" often became patrons in their own right. In addition a high level of anxiety is introduced into party politics by the almost continuous electioneering atmosphere of the Federal Republic. Within every four year period there is one federal election and 11 state elections, each of which is interpreted in federal terms. Such uncertainty of majority, the short-lived nature of electoral success at the federal level (witness the resignations of Erhard and Brandt so soon after spectacular electoral victories), and the many possibilities for political frustration lead the parties to seek control over unpredictable areas. For example, the CDU/CSU has feared sabotage by the broadcasting media; the SPD has feared bureaucratic sabotage of its programs. Polarization can then be reinforced, perhaps even generated by electoral anxieties. An atmosphere of electoral uncertainty can lead to an "over-activation" of the political parties.

The infiltration of party into administration *within limits* has its advantages. It helps introduce policy-relevant knowledge into party discussion and disseminates public service values within the parties. Consequently West German parties benefit from a reservoir of talent unavailable in Britain where political and administrative careers are sharply demarcated. In this way the tendency for the parties to remain primarily instruments of government with a genuinely broad focus—rather than mere pressure groups or ideological clubs—is reinforced. The British political parties by contrast remain more closely identified with particular sectional interests. Career incentives offered by the parties have helped to stabilize them and, by generating a desire on the part of members to see their party in government, reinforced the trend to Volksparteien. Administrative views and styles are conveyed in a novel way into party and parliamentary settings. There is, however, no serious evidence that the "party-book" administration has been at the expense of the professional qualities of the bureaucracy; complaints that administrative quality has been sacrificed to political reliability are few. *Filzokratie* is, therefore, a different phenomenon to the "machine politics" of American cities. Party patronage was introduced in Germany into a system with a long-established professional administration, and its strengthening after 1945 was combined with a high degree of continuity in the administrative sphere. Well-defined rules operate to protect both political and administrative ethics with neither side expecting administrative rules to be broken solely for reasons of political pressure or expediency. Political and administrative styles are interfused as in the U.S., but on terms that give precedence to public service values. The chief contrast with Britain and the U.S. is that the relation between party and bureaucracy is shaped by the state tradition. The mutual accommodation of party and state bureaucracy was realized by combining retention of the traditional social and political privileges of the administrator (with consequences for the political process) with modification but not displacement of the career principle in the interests of party control. Party attempts to use the public service for welfare functions or to extend direct controls were matched by transfer of administrative values into the parties themselves. Consequently public service ethics remain strong. The product is neither party nor bureaucratic dominance but a reciprocal influence mediated by the state which, within limits, is to the advantage of the new political system. These limits are defined by the continuing possibility for effective public control over the exercise of power. One factor which has helped to mitigate dangers to public control is the sheer heterogeneity in terms of divergence of interest and political conception within the public service (for example, the phenomenon of radical teachers in the SPD).

Such a system of interfused political and administrative styles does have its problems. For example, there is not the clear role conceptions on the part of politicians and administrators to be found in Britain, although this is probably offset by the accumulation at political levels of organizational and professional policy skills to provide policy initiatives. At political levels there is a greater capacity to think in terms of well-defined policy objectives and to critically evaluate programs designed to achieve them. West German governments possess a willingness and capacity to plan their operations not found in Britain. A further problem is the inevitable tension between political interest in rewards for supporters versus administrative ethics. "Marginal politicization" is to be found in most policy areas. A classic example is the so-called "mayoral competition" within the states for priorities and resources. For example, it is difficult for administrators in CDU states to resist the pressure of powerful CDU mayors for particular favors. In addition there are always figures who have not adequately internalized the "rules" particularly when these are as complex as in West Germany.

There remains a sense of loyalty to the administrative profession and to its procedural expertise which involves legal and technical considerations beyond party political calculations. Party politicization is further limited by two other factors. First, the doctrine of the Rechtsstaat turns large areas of administration into a quasi-judicial process, a technical exercise for professionals. Here the decision-making process become semi-autonomous and the notion of responsibility for application of the law (subject to the administrative courts) using judicial criteria and methods competes with the doctrine of ministerial responsibility. In other words the doctrine of the Rechtsstaat produces the notion of an administrative sphere where political intervention is an "intrusion" (Mayer and Ulle, 1969: 133-134). Second, whilst public service law recognizes that German officials are servants of the state, it does not identify this state as a Parteienstaat. German officials are enjoined to serve "the whole people" in terms of the public good. There exists, therefore, the possibility of conflict of loyalties between the state and the government of the day. Such a possibility is reduced in Britain by the fact that civil servants are servants of the Crown and thus do not necessarily have a higher loyalty than to the ministers of the day who are ministers of the Crown (Ridley, 1975: 453-455). Despite these restrictions on party politicization, party as a focus of loyalty has become increasingly important in West German bureaucracy and represents a particularly important part of the complex of the official's working world. However, it would be a mistake to see party as the only or necessarily even the major loyalty of the official.

PARTY STATE AND ELITE ACCOMMODATION

The Federal Republic is neither an example of straightforward majority rule nor an example of rule by mutual agreement and political accommodation in the form outlined in the theory of "consociational democracy."[17] Clearly pure majority rule is rendered difficult, it not impossible, by the nature of the federal system, which requires complex consensus building through largely private bargaining between federal and state bureaucracies and party groups at federal and regional levels. The recent debate about the Bundesrat well reflects the tension between mutual agreement and majority rule as principles of decision-making. Majority rule is also qualified by a corporatist tradition which legitimates a powerful role for major interest groups. One is struck by the predominance of a different pattern of decision-making in the Federal Republic to that in Britain. There is a style of elite accommodation which stresses cooperative strategies of problem solving. Such a style is not to be explained in terms of "consociational theory" and is not particularly associated with "consociational devices."

Historical tradition reinforces customs of managing political conflicts by negotiation amongst parties and interest groups (typically in private)— rather than by open political contest and parliamentary majorities (Lehmbruch, 1968: 204). A similar tradition finds expression in Austria and

Switzerland. There remains a strand in German political culture which views party cooperation as a precondition for impartial, rational, and just decision-making and party conflict as prejudicial to consensus. This view is reinforced by the integrative values stressed by the state tradition which, at the turn of the century, had greater credence when writers like Richard Thoma (1930) and Max Weber (1958) were suggesting that class, regional, and religious cleavages made Anglo-Saxon majoritarianism a dangerous device for Germany. Dahrendorf's (1968: 278) term "cartel of elites"—referring to an unwillingness of elites to take initiatives and a disposition to avoid individual responsibility—is helpful in pinpointing a sense of caution and mutual forbearance characterizing relations between party elites. Another traditional strategy of conflict resolution is the arbitration of conflict by some supposedly superior and "neutral" authority, traditionally the bureaucracy and the law, both again identified with the state. Much of the significance of the Constitutional Court today stems from this tradition. Both of these traditions continue to qualify the exercise of majority rule. There remains strong support for cooperative strategies as opposed to competitive strategies of electoral competition and majority rule. Opposition behavior within the Bundestag is indicative. It has typically been cooperative rather than competitive (Friedrich, 1975). Despite the image of confrontation characterizing the first (1949-1953) and sixth (1969-1972) Bundestags, the reality has been one of legislative cooperation in the privacy of committees and other private meetings. In the case of the vast majority of legislation it is difficult to identify which party is responsible for which section or provision. Within the Bundestag the distinction of government and opposition becomes blurred. Institutional factors encourage oppositions to use strategies of cooperation and bargaining to exert significant influence on legislation.

Another modification to majoritarianism is introduced by the strength and style of interest group politics which is also influenced by the state tradition as well as by a corporatist tradition which goes back to the concepts of functional representation associated with the *Ständestaat*. *Konzertierte Aktion* ("concerted action")—a regular meeting of federal government representatives with management and union representatives to discuss prospective economic development including wage-price guidelines—may be much less formalized than its Austrian equivalent. There are, nevertheless, similarities between the two which distinguish them from their Anglo-Saxon equivalents. In both countries the chambers are quite unlike their British or American equivalents and represent a notable degree of organization and coordination of economic life. Interest groups are characterized by a high level of bureaucratization and centralization which provide their leaderships with considerable independence for negotiation. Above all there is a shared conception amongst such leaders that mutual accommodation is preferable to a stronger government role in economic affairs. There is a shared interest (which is not dependent simply on shared goals) in maintaining an economic policy-making system which permits such a high level of interest group autonomy and participation. Hence a rather different ideal of a pluralistic society is encapsulated in the term *Sozialpartner*. Interest groups see each other as "partners in society" rather than simply as antagonists. In other words interest group politics is characterized (more than in Britain or the U.S.) by a preference for cooperative strategies.

In so far as ideas are important in politics, the form and practice of government and the nature of the pluralistic process in Western Germany as in France are not to be understood without reference to the state. By contrast to France the West German state tradition has seen two major changes.

In the first place integration of party and state has bestowed upon the parties a privileged position in the pluralistic process. Nevertheless it is clear from this paper that the Parteienstaat remains an object of controversy. The Right, influenced by the traditional dualism of state and society, decries the effects of the parties on the state; the Left bemoans the effects of the state on the parties; whilst liberal intellectuals fear that dominance of party perspectives will restrict political horizons. The key difference to France is that all these critics can agree than an integration of party and state has taken place. They are just criticizing the consequences from different perspectives.

Of equal importance is the influence of the state on interest groups. Legitimacy of interest group power (not bestowed by the Basic Law) is sought by those groups adopting styles and behavior patterns consistent with the state. For example, the term "interest group" is dropped in favor of the more neutral *Verband* which typically "moralizes" its interests either by naked identification of these interests with the common good or by disguising its interests. Indeed many groups assume a semi-public character as administrators of state regulations. The legacy of the state seems therefore somewhat ambiguous. Identification with the state by an interest may only be a useful precondition for using the state as an instrument for the satisfaction of one's desires. It would seem to encourage the dangers of dissimulation as well as of conservatism. At the same time the very process of identification has implications for values and style. Assimilation of the state tradition by the parties and emulation of that tradition by interest goup leadership provide an integrating influence within the pluralistic process and facilitate a more collaborative style of government-interest group relations in which the emphasis is on partnership. There is a sense of acting for the "whole," of having a general responsibility, within of course the constraint of carrying one's members along with commitments. The Sozialpartner (partners in society) pursue a strongly pragmatic and instrumental style, downgrading ideology in favor of Sachlichkeit (objectivity, practicality, realism) illustrated by the role of economic and statistical experts. Issues tend to be seen in technical terms. By contrast, in France significant groups stand opposed to the state. In Germany these factors along with the permeable nature of administration have led to a more thorough dissemination of public service values, a stronger ethic of social responsibility, than in either Britain or France. As a consequence the political system appears to its radical critics as particularly monolithic and hostile to dissent (witness the Radicals Decree). It is easy to interpret such a cooperative indeed corporatist style of pluralistic politics in conspiratorial terms. The ideological dimension of politics is weakened whilst political opportunism particularly within officialdom appears to be strengthened. One consequence is a politics of centrality, of "constructive" rather than simply "disjointed" incrementalism as competing actors in the pluralistic process are united by a sense of common interests (Smith, 1976). Whilst such a pluralistic process may lack "drama" compared to its British counterpart, it does provide slow and secure change. In fact German interest groups are no less powerful than their American or British equivalents. Indeed their rationalized structure, sheer organizational capacity, and professional competence make them very formidable forces. The crucial factor is not their power but their use of that power. "Concerted Action" (Konzertierte Aktion) as a method of economic management has always been a more practicable proposition in Germany than the tripartite structure of NEDC (the National Economic Development Council) in Britain.

A second major change has been a shift in the philosophy of the state away from a mercantilist tradition to the neoliberalism of the social market economy. This faith in the institutions and functioning of the market economy has strengthened the collaborative style in economic policy-making. Nevertheless, the concept of the *Sozialstaat* (which is supposed to be recognized in Articles 20 (1) and 28 (1) of the Basic Law) is an explicit rejection of "laissez-faire" in social policy and is a point of convergence with the French concept of the state; the state is expected to provide comprehensive public services. Despite this "public service" state German administrative style tends to be less abrasive and self-confident than its

French counterpart. Neoliberalism has combined with the legalism of the Rechtsstaat and of course with historical memories to introduce a certain modesty into the exercise of governmental power. The nature of the pluralist process particularly the values and style of its participants has, however, facilitated the governmental role more than in Britain. A sense of shared responsibility—combined with the presence of organizational and policy skills at the top, produced by the interaction of political and administrative careers—helps explain the generally better performance of German than of British governments in recent years.

The transcendental and sovereign German state of the past has been largely demytholigized and is seen today primarily as a "public service" state. However, the concepts of both the Sozialstaat and the Rechtsstaat are related to the traditional view that the state is a moral agency. In the case of the Rechtsstaat both its material contents (that is, the basic rights of the constitution) and its formal procedures are seen as pursuing moral ends, whilst the Sozialstaat represents a continuing belief in the desirability of public regulation. The German concept of the state lends to terms like Rechtsstaat and Sozialstaat quite different meanings than their British equivalents: the rule of law and the welfare state. It is only possible to understand the peculiar importance of law in West Germany in terms of the identification of law and the state. According to the concept of the Rechtsstaat, the activities of the state are defined and controlled by law. It is in law that the moral functions of the state are expressed and guarded. Hence the Rechtsstaat has become more than a formal and procedural code. Clearly this concept is quite different from the formal concept of the rule of law and explains the German passion for codification, the major role of the Federal Constitutional Court, and the dominance of jurists within the administration. Likewise the concept of the Sozialstaat is much broader than welfare state. Not surprisingly the British concept of the welfare state has perjorative overtones implying the erosion of individual responsibility. In Britain public services are largely a response to erratic uncoordinated political pressures. There is no conception of the state with a general and inherent responsibility for the provision of public services. In the context of German history the concept of the welfare state (*Wohlfahrtsstaat*) has a conservative and authoritarian implication referring simply to the provision of social security. The modern concept of the Sozialstaat legitimates not only a public service and interventionist role for the state but also social participation and partnership of interests in economic and social affairs. It raises questions of codetermination in industry, the form of economic organization, tax policy and policies for wealth redistribution. At the same time its generality makes its interpretation the subject of much dispute with the Right, which stresses the welfare aspects, and the Left, which emphasizes the partnership aspect of the Sozialstaat. Its major importance lies in its rejection of the concept of the "neutral" state in favor of an interlocking of state and society. Public regulation of private interests is complemented by a role for such interests within the state.

The chief legacy of the state is a sense that political and administrative actors have a moral function and must seek to embody the common welfare and a concern for public order in the widest sense. Hence these actors tend, sometimes deceptively, to "moralize" about their activities. Government is not viewed in the instrumental or functional terms found in Britain or the United States; it has a special mystique. A further legacy of the state is a continuing respect for objective and rational assessment as the basis for the authoritative determination of the public interest. This respect is reflected in a faith in the expert and in arbitration of conflict from above. The divisive potential of pluralism is further restrained by the emphasis on the unity of public powers which goes with the state. It is, for example, not possible to understand the relatively smooth working of West German federalism without reference to the legacy of the state. A final legacy is the continuing emphasis on the special role of the Beamte in public life. The traditional view that the Beamte is in a special relationship of service and loyalty to the state is still reflected in a highly independent ethic and ethos of service which has been widely disseminated through German life.

The state and its emphasis on executive power is the common factor which—unlike the Weimar Republic—fuses party and bureaucracy together. It does so by interlocking them on terms which give the parties a formal ascendancy and produce the term Parteienstaat. In addition, the state tradition influences the nature of intraparty relations (witness the imperative mandate issue where the state tradition clashed with a plebiscitary democratic tradition) and shapes the pluralistic process where it combines with an important corporatist tradition. Attachment of the major parties to the state tradition is facilitated by a federal system (Bundesstaat) which allows the opposition to participate as state (Land) governments and members of the Bundesrat in a share of state power. The issue of abuse of the Bundesrat reflects in fact its ambiguity as the representative of the Bundesstaat and as a body composed of party members. A similar type of ambiguity plagues the bureaucracy and finds its expression in the debate about *Filzokratie.*

It has in the past been fashionable to interpret the continental "state" tradition as a burden for democratic development. Whilst this burden has been evident in the German past, it is today more apparent in France than in the Federal Republic where it has been assimilated to produce what might be described as a "public service democracy." Moreover in both cases the concept of the state imposes a sense of higher purpose on the processes of compromise by bargaining which are a normal feature of the pluralistic process. In France respect for such purposes is more often imposed (albeit within the constraints of political realities) on recalcitrant interests by governments with a will to govern; in the Federal Republic there is a tendency for such perspectives to be assimilated by the interests themselves who have sought legitimacy and power by acquiring official status. There is, in other words, more respect for unitary conceptions of the public interest, whether stressing certain common shared ends or corporate community ends. By contrast "stateless societies" (the Anglo-American democracies) tend towards more individualistic and utilitarian concepts of the public interest in terms of the competition of particular interests. Both France and West Germany seem to possess a more structured process of pluralism than the Anglo-American democracies and more ability to avoid the debilitating effects of "stagnant pluralism."

NOTES

1. According to Lijphart (1974: 79) "consociational democracies" are characterized by elite accommodation institutionalized in "consociational devices" (grand coalitions, coalition pacts, and commissions, *Proporz* in personnel policy). Today the Federal Republic does not have a severely fragmented political culture in which such devices might aid stability; nor does its style of elite accommodation depend on such devices.

2. As a consequence of the election (by secret parliamentary vote) of Ernst Albrecht (CDU) as minister-president of Lower Saxony, the SPD/FDP lost control over the procedure of the Bundesrat and its majority in the arbitration committee which works out compromises between Bundestag and Bundesrat on controversial issues. After the CDU/CSU emerged from the 1976 federal election as the largest Bundestag party further problems with the Bundesrat were expected.

3. Normally government bills are submitted to the Bundesrat before the Bundestag and the Bundesrat is given six weeks to respond.

4. Between 1969 and April 1974 some 40 government bills were significantly modified as a result of Bundesrat proposals in the arbitration committee. The three major vetoes of the 1972-1976 period were the proposals for an increase of the value-added tax in 1975 and for a betterment levy and the federal government's bill on exclusion of radicals from the public service. Observers began to speak of de facto all-party government.

5. A useful source for politicians' views on this issue is Schindler (1974).

6. There are three types of public servants: *Beamte* (whose special duties to the state are compensated for by numerous privileges including security of tenure and noncontributory pensions); *Angestellte* (employed on a contractual basis); and *Arbeiter* (workers). In reality the distinction between officials *(Beamte)* and employees *(Angestellte)* has become blurred.

7. The so-called "Radicals Decree" refers to a decision of the Minister-President's Conference in January 1972 which sought to specify criteria to guide exclusion of radicals from the public service. By early 1975 there were already over 400 documented cases of exclusion.

8. Of those questioned in the administration of Bremen (Senatskanzlei Bremen, 1972), 44% chose "party membership and political reliability" as a factor which played the largest role in appointments; 50% gave primacy to "personal connections." In a general survey, Luhmann and Mayntz (1973) found that 12% of those questioned (19% in the higher civil service) regarded membership in the "right" party or party political activity as a guarantee of success.

9. These included State Secretary Pöhl (a former journalist), Geske (head of the European division and former SPD official), and Lahnstein (head of the central division). Apel was publicly rebuked by the Ministry's Personnel Council for allowing "personal connections" to influence appointments at the expense of merit.

10. A good example is the Federal Press and Information Office, a former CDU stronghold, whose staff of Beamte increased from 129 in 1969 to 218 in 1975. Debate within its personnel council about appointments became strongly party political.

11. From the bureau *(Referat)* level down good relations with the personnel council are often more important than hierarchical relations for promotion (Luhmann and Mayntz, 1973: 253).

12. These categories refer to the typical situation. In fact there is some variation with Bavaria, Baden-Würtemberg, Hamburg, and Bremen not establishing such positions.

13. Interviews were realized in 65% of cases, that is, 483 out of 743 positions.

14. It is wrong to equate party membership with enthusiastic party commitment; the latter can also exist without the former.

15. In the early years of the CSU small active groups within the Bavarian administration played a key role in the party's development. Hans Ehard as minister-president and party chairman (1949-1955) preferred to direct the party from the State Chancellery and through party members in the administration rather than from party headquarters (Mintzel, 1972: 219).

16. In the case of the second television service, Adenauer's attempt to establish a federal station was rejected by the court.

17. Lehmbruch (1967) distinguishes between a competitive pattern of conflict management of which the fundamental device is the majority principle (such as Britain and the U.S.) and a noncompetitive "cartelized" pattern that works by amicable agreement (such as Austria and Switzerland).

REFERENCES

ALMOND, G. A. (1956) "Comparative political systems." J. of Politics 18; 391-409.
ARMSTRONG, J. A. (1973) The European Administrative Elite. New Jersey: Princeton Univ. Press.
BARTHEL, W. (1973) "Der Parteibuch-Staat." Der Stern 40.
BAUMANN, G. [ed.] (1974) Bericht über Deutschland. Druffel Verlag.
BERMBACH, U. (1970) "Probleme des Parteienstaates, Der Fall Littmann." Zeitschrift für Parlamentsfragen 3 (October): 342-363.
BURKETT, T. (1975) Parties and Elections in West Germany. London: Hurst.
CDU im Landtag (1974) Bildungspolitik. Kiel: Landtag.
DAALDER, H. (1966) "Parties, elites and political developments in Western Europe," pp. 43-78 in J. LaPalombara and M. Weiner (eds.) Political Parties and Political Development. New Jersey: Princeton Univ. Press.
DAHRENDORF, R. (1968) Society and Democracy in Germany. London: Weidenfeld & Nicolson.
DYSON, K.H.F. (1975a) "Anti-communism in the Federal Republic of Germany: the case of the Berufsverbot." Parliamentary Affairs (Spring): 51-67.
――― (1975b) "Left-wing political extremism and the problem of tolerance in Western Germany." Government and Opposition 3 (Summer): 306-331.
――― (1975c) "Improving policymaking in Bonn." J. of Management Studies 2 (May): 157-174.
――― (1974) "The German federal chancellor's office." Political Q. (June).
EASTON, D. (1953) The Political System. New York: Knopf.
ELLWEIN, T. (1973) Das Regierungssystem der Bundesrepublik Deutschland. Opladen: Westdeutscher Verlag.
――― and R. ZOLL (1973) Berufsbeamtentum―Anspruch und Wirklichkeit. Düsseldorf: Bertelsmann.
ESCHENBURG, T. (1974) "Der bürokratische Rückhalt," pp. 64-94 in R. Löwenthal and H. P. Schwarz, Die Zweite Republik. Stuttgart: Seewald.
――― (1961) Amterpatronage. Stuttgart.
FRIEDRICH, M. (1975) "Opposition im Deutschen Bundestag. Phasen oppositionellen Verhaltens 1949-1972," in H. Oberreuter (ed.) Parlamentarische Opposition. Hamburg: Hoffmann & Campe.
Fulton Committee (1968) Report on the Civil Service. London: H.M.S.O.
GREBING, H. (1972) "Volksrepräsentation and identitäre Demokratie." Politische Vierteljahresschrift 13: 162.
GROTTIAN, P. (1974) Strukturprobleme staatlicher Planung. Hamburg: Hoffmann & Campe.
HEIDENHEIMER, A. J. (1958) "Federalism and the party system: the case of West Germany." Amer. Pol. Sci. Rev. 3: 809-828.
HENNIS, W. (1973) Die missverstandene Demokratie. Freiburg: Herder.
――― (1968) Verfassung und Verfassungswirklichkeit: ein deutsches Problem. Tübinten: J.C.B. Mohr.
HESS, A. (1976) "Statistische Daten und Trends zur Verbeamtung der Parlamente im Bund und Ländern." Zeitschrift für Parlamentsfragen 1 (April): 34-42.
JOHNSON, N. (1968) "Western Germany," pp. 134-149 in F. Ridley (ed.) Specialists and Generalists. London: Allen & Unwin.

KALTEFLEITER, W. and A. VEEN (1974) "Zwischen freiem und imperativem Mandat." Zeitschrift für Parlamentsfragen 2 (July): 246-267.
LAUFER, H. (1970) "Der Bundesrat als Instrument der Opposition?" Zeitschrift für Parlamentsfragen 3 (October): 318-341.
LEHMBRUCH, G. (1968) "The ambiguous coalition in West Germany." Government and Opposition 3 (Summer): 181-204.
––– (1967) "A non-competitive pattern of conflict management in liberal democracies: the case of Switzerland, Austria, and Lebanon." Paper delivered at Seventh World Congress of the Internatl. Pol. Sci. Assn., Brussels.
LEIBHOLZ, G. (1967) Strukturprobleme der modernen Demokratie. Third ed. Karlsruhe: V. F. Müller.
LIJPHART, A. (1974) "Consociational democracy," pp. 70-106 in K. McRae (ed.) Consociational Democracy: Political Accommodation in Segmented Societies. Toronto: McClelland & Stewart.
LUHMANN, N. and R. MAYNTZ (1973) Personal im öffentlichen Dienst. Baden-Baden: Nomos Verlagsgesellschaft.
MAYER, F. and C. H. ULE (1969) Staats-und Verwaltungsrecht in Rheinland-Pfalz. Stuttgart: Richard Boorberg Verlag.
MAYNTZ, R. and F. SCHARPF [eds.] (1973) Planungsorganisation. München: Piper Verlag.
MERKL, P. H. (1959) "Executive-legislative federalism in West Germany." Amer. Pol. Sci. Rev. 3: 732-741.
MINTZEL, A. (1972) "Die CSU in Bayern." Politische Viertaljahresschrift 13: 205-243.
NETTL, J. P. (1968) "The state as a conceptual variable." World Politics 4 (July): 559-592.
PUTNAM, R. D. (1973) "The political attitudes of senior civil servants in Western Europe: a preliminary report." British J. of Pol. Sci. 3.
RASCHKE, J. (1974) Innerparteiliche Opposition: Die Linke in der Berliner SPD. Hamburg: Hoffmann & Campe.
RIDLEY, F. F. (1975) "Responsibility and the official: forms and ambiguities." Government and Opposition 4: 444-472.
RIGGS, F. W. (1964) Administration in Developing Countries: The Theory of Prismatic Society. Boston: Houghton-Mifflin.
SCHELSKY, H. (1974) "A German dilemma." Encounter (February).
SCHEUING, D. H. [ed.] (1974) Der Bundesratt als Verfassungsorgan und politische Kraft. Bad Honnef: Neue Darmstadter Verlagsanstalt.
SCHINDLER, P. (1974) "Missbrauch des Bundesrates? Dokumentation einer aktuellen Auseinandersetzung." Zeitschrift für Parlamentsfragen 2 (July): 157-166.
SCHMIDT, E. (1971) Ordnungsfaktor oder Gegenmacht: Die politische Rolle der Gewerkschaften. Frankfurt: Suhrkamp Verlag.
SCHMOLLINGER, H. W. (1975) "Die Berliner Wahlen zum Abgeordnetenhaus und zu den Bezirksverordnetenversammlungen vom 2 Marz 1957." Zeitschrift für Parlamentsfragen 4 (December): 446-464.
––– (1974) "Abhängig Beschäftigte in Parteien der Bundesrepublik: Einflussmöglich von Arbeitern, Angestellten und Beamten." Zeitschrift für Parlamentsfragen 1 (March): 58-90.
SEEMANN, K. (1975) Entzaubertes Bundeskanzleramt. Verlag Politisches Archiv.

Senatskanzlei Bremen (1972) Organisationssoziologische Untersuchung der bremischen Verwaltung. Bremen: Rathaus.

SMITH, G. (1976) "The politics of centrality: the case of Western Germany." Government and Opposition 3: 387-407.

SONTHEIMER, K. and W. BLEEK (1973) Abschied vom Berufsbeamtentum? Hamburg: Hoffmann & Campe.

STEINKEMPER, B. (1974) Klassische und Politische Bürokraten in der Ministerialverwaltung der Bundesrepublik Deutschland. Köln: Carl Heymanns Verlag.

Studienkommission für die Reform des öffentlichen Dienstrechts. Bericht der Kommission (1973). Baden-Baden: Nomos Verlagsgesellschaft.

THAYSEN, U. (1975) Parlamentarisches Regierungssystem in der Bundesrepublik Deutschland. Hamburg: Landeszentrale für politische Bildung.

THOMA, R. (1930) "Das Reich als Demokratie," 195 in Handbuch des Deutschen Staatsrechts vol. 1. Tübingen.

TRAUTMANN, G. (1971) "Parteienstaatliche Verfassung und freies Mandat." Zeitschrift für Parlamentsfragen 1 (April): 54-69.

VARAIN, H. J. (1964) Parteien und Verbände: Eine Studie über Ihren Aufau, ihre Verflechtung und ihr Wirken in Schleswig-Holstein 1945-1958. Opladen: Westdeutscher Verlag.

WEBER, M. (1958) Gesammelte politische Schriften. Tübingen.

WILDENMANN, R. (1968) Eliten in der Bundesrepublik. Eine sozialwissenschaftliche Untersuchung über Einstellungen führender Positionsträger zur Politik und Demokratie. Mannheim: Tabellenband.

WILLIAMS, A. (1976) Broadcasting and Democracy in Western Germany. Bradford: Bradford Univ. Press.

ZAPF, W. (1966) Wandlungen der deutschen Elite. München.

KENNETH DYSON, lecturer in politics at the University of Liverpool, is secretary of the Association for the Study of German Politics. He received his undergraduate and postgraduate degrees from the London School of Economics. His articles have appeared in such scholarly journals as Government and Opposition, Parliamentary Affairs, Political Studies, Local Government Studies, Political Quarterly, *and the* Journal of Management Studies. *He is now writing a book on pluralism and the state in Western Europe.*